PHalarope Books are designed specifically for the amateur naturalist. These volumes represent excellence in natural history publishing. Most books in the PHalarope series are based on a nature course or program at the college or adult education level or are sponsored by a museum or nature center. Each PHalarope book reflects the author's teaching ability as well as writing ability. Among the books:

The Amateur Naturalist's Handbook
Vinson Brown

Botany in the Field: An Introduction to Plant Communities for the Amateur Naturalist
Jane Scott

A Field Guide to the Familiar: Learning to Observe the Natural World
Gale Lawrence

Insect Life: A Field Entomology Manual for the Amateur Naturalist
Ross H. Arnett, Jr., Richard L. Jacques, Jr.

A Natural History Notebook of North American Animals
National Museum of Natural History, Canada

Owls: An Introduction for the Amateur Naturalist
Gordon Dee Alcorn

The Plant Observer's Guidebook: A Field Botany Manual for the Amateur Naturalist
Charles E. Roth

Suburban Wildflowers: An Introduction to the Common Wildflowers of Your Back Yard and Local Park
Richard Headstrom

Suburban Wildlife: An Introduction to the Common Animals of Your Back Yard and Local Park
Richard Headstrom

Thoreau's Method: A Handbook for Nature Study
David Pepi

Trees: An Introduction to Trees and Forest Ecology for the Amateur Naturalist
Laurence C. Walker

The Western Birdwatcher: An Introduction to Birding in the American West
Kevin J. Zimmer

The Wildlife Observer's Guidebook
Charles E. Roth, Massachusetts Audubon Society

Wood Notes: A Companion and Guide for Birdwatchers
Richard H. Wood

The Sky Observer's Guidebook
Charles E. Roth

Lola Oberman

ILLUSTRATED BY JOY SWAN

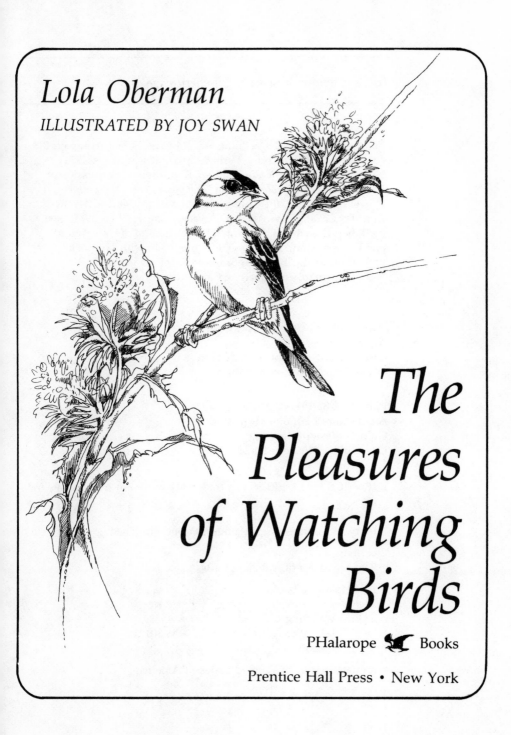

The Pleasures of Watching Birds

PHalarope Books

Prentice Hall Press • New York

To Ted, whose presence is on every page

Published by Prentice Hall Press
A Division of Simon & Schuster, Inc.
Gulf + Western Building
One Gulf + Western Plaza
New York, NY 10023

PRENTICE HALL PRESS is a trademark of Simon & Schuster, Inc.

Library of Congress Cataloging-in-Publication Data

Oberman, Lola.
  The pleasures of watching birds.

  (A PHalarope book)
  Includes index.
  1. Bird watching   I. Title.
QL677.5.024   1986   598'.07'234   85-30121
ISBN 0-13-681305-4

Manufactured in the United States of America

10 9 8 7 6 5 4 3 2 1

CONTENTS

FOREWORD

BIRDING IS THE HOBBY FOR THE YOUNG AT HEART—THOSE
of all ages who would enjoy the out-of-doors, those
eager for new experiences, for widening horizons, and
new friendships—those who look forward to a lifetime
of enjoyment and satisfaction. The birder develops an
awareness and appreciation for the ever-changing natural scene of which he is a part. He does not need to
become an expert in order to enjoy his hobby; but tens
of thousands of birders become proficient enough to
participate each year in personal or group projects that
contribute new information about our avian resource
and its relation to the changing environment. Orni-
thology is the only science in which the amateur plays
such an important role.

The professionalism of birding today is in marked
contrast to my boyhood experience in the early thirties.
At that time there was no adequate field guide, there
were no records or tapes of bird songs and calls, and
there were few bird clubs. A birder with his 3-power

opera glass was a curiosity, and at times even the recipient of ridicule. A decade later, during the war, we
attracted suspicion when birding with optics along the
coast, and frequently resorted to telling curious passers-
by that we were watching for submarines.

Today, literally millions of birders carry field guides
and prism binoculars. The 1980 *National Survey of Fishing, Hunting, and Wildlife-Associated Recreation*, published
by the U.S. Fish and Wildlife Service and the Bureau of
the Census, reported that 83.2 million citizens over fifteen years of age engaged in some form of noncon-
sumptive activity in which wildlife was the primary
purpose. This was nearly five times the number of
sportsmen who went hunting that year.

Along with the increase in birding activity has been
the improvement in birding aids such as binoculars,
telescopes, field guides, and reference material. There
are now detailed bird reference books for almost every
state and province, a wealth of fine, illustrated field
identification guides covering nearly every country on
earth, guides to bird behavior, guides to nests and eggs,
national and state guides to the best bird-finding local-
ities, and even a guide to 850 North American bird clubs.

Even after fifty years of birding, I learn something
new about birds virtually every time I go out for a few
hours. I know you will, too, whatever your particular
interest may be. Some of the facets of birding that continue to fascinate me are the regularity with which mi-
gratory birds return each spring at approximately the
same date; the effects of weather on bird migration; the
ability of long-distance migrants to find their way to the
same wintering grounds in the tropics each autumn and
return to the same woodlot in the United States or Canada each spring; the stability of populations of many
species over the decades despite massive changes in the
environment; the songs and call notes that are distinctive of each species; the response of birds to artificial
feeding stations; and the scores of species that can be

found during the course of a year in a single suburban garden.

Birding, like sports, can be active or passive. It can be competitive or not, as the participant chooses. It may be enjoyed from a hospital or kitchen window, by commuters on the way to work, by farmers in the field or fishermen in the stream, and especially by vacationers and retirees.

Lola Oberman is eminently qualified to present the thrills of birding to the public. She regularly leads field trips for the Maryland Ornithological Society and the Audubon Naturalist Society; she is a past president of the Montgomery County chapter of the Maryland Ornithological Society and a contributing editor of *Audubon Naturalist News*. She has combined her ornithological expertise with her literary talent to show how birding has sharpened her powers of observation and to explain how this hobby has changed her daily life.

This book will whet your appetite by revealing many ways in which you can enjoy birds in the immediate vicinity of your home, how you can meet other birders, including the local experts, how you can become involved in group activities, and how you can get help with your identification problems. Above all, it will impress you with the infinite variety of birding experiences that await you at your own window or in the nearest small park.

Chandler S. Robbins

PREFACE

IF, AS THOREAU BELIEVED, "MOST MEN LEAD LIVES OF QUIET desperation," it is because they have not learned the soothing and restorative powers of nature. This book is a testimonial to those powers, and an encouragement to readers to take time out from their busy lives to contemplate the remarkably busy and endlessly fascinating lives of birds.

If you are among those fortunate souls who have already succumbed to the lure of birds, you need no encouragement. You know the rewards: the excitement of pursuit, the joy of discovery, the satisfaction of sharing nature's gifts with comrades, the deep sense of physical and mental well-being that ensures a sound sleep at the end of a day on the trail. You may recognize yourself in some of these pages, for this book is about the watchers as well as the watched, recounting personal adventures of the kind that are shared whenever birders get together. You may laugh with me at our foibles and frailties, our frustrations and embarrassments, and our classic blunders in the field. You may also relive in memory some of your most cherished moments in birding and feel a touch of envy for those who have these bright new experiences ahead of them.

If you are a newcomer to the field, you will find comfort in the assurance that beginners, like recent converts to a religion, are treated with tender, loving care by the old hands. They are aware, even if you are not, that you are embarking on a new way of life that will forever change your outlook and even your daily habits. In these pages you may find answers to questions you are too shy to ask: How should you behave in the presence of seasoned birders? Is there a code of conduct? How should you prepare for a birding trip? What should you wear? What books should you buy? Would you dare go on a Christmas Count? To help guide you, I offer not a rigid list of dos and don'ts but anecdotes that reveal whys and wherefores so that it all begins to make sense. Myths and misconceptions may melt away as you read of the personal experiences of others. You may be able to avoid some of their mistakes—or at least to relax in the knowledge that to err is human, especially in the pursuit of birds, for they can confound even the most expert observers.

If you are among the vast and growing number of benefactors who maintain feeding stations and enjoy watching the birds that gather in their back yards, this book will encourage you to spend more time at your window. Marvelous things are happening out there when your back is turned. Even if you never go afield in search of new birds, you have a world of adventure within sight of your house. In fourteen years, I have counted ninety-two species on or flying over our rather typical suburban property. Who knows how many more I might have seen if I had spent less time at my typewriter and more time at the window? In the section titled "Views from the Window," you will find intimate portraits of some of my visitors, shedding light on unusual aspects of their behavior. Elsewhere in the book, you may pick up useful hints on coping with "Troublesome Birds" as well as ". . . Birds in Trouble."

If you are but an occasional and casual watcher of birds, some of the stories in this collection will impress upon you the everyday wonders you are missing and impel you to take a closer look at the birds that come your way—to stand and stare, to marvel at their beauty and cleverness and the way they organize their lives. And if you have been baffled by the strange behavior of a dedicated birder—perhaps someone near and dear to you—this book may give you a measure of understanding. Birding, as you will see, is not just a hobby to fill in the empty hours. It is a way of life, in tune with the total natural scene. Call it an addiction if you like; but it is a benign addiction from which great blessings flow.

This book is intended for all those who are delighted with, fascinated by, or merely curious about birds. It requires no special background, no prior knowledge of the subject. It requires only a quiet evening, or a day when pouring rain or gale-force winds prevent you from going out to seek birding adventures of your own.

First-hand adventures are always the best, of course. But you may find some vicarious enjoyment in reading of memorable adventures that have brought me pleasure, pain, and laughter. They may stimulate the recall of similar experiences of your own, or they may hold forth hope of future pleasures. But be forewarned: There are stories here that you will never duplicate in a lifetime of birding, for the variables in nature are infinite. So are the variables in human nature. And just as each foray into the field is unique and individual, so are the insights each of us brings to the experience.

I hope this book will give you new insights that will enhance your enjoyment in watching birds.

Acknowledgments

MOST OF THE MATERIAL IN THIS BOOK APPEARED OVER THE past eight years as "Notes from Melody Lane" in the *Audubon Naturalist News,* published by the Audubon Naturalist Society of the Central Atlantic States, in Chevy Chase, Maryland. I am grateful to loyal readers and to a succession of patient editors, especially Pat Eden, Kathy Rushing, and Pat Cassimatis, who were most tolerant about deadlines when I was off on the birding trail. Special thanks go to Mary Bowers, the editor of *Bird Watcher's Digest,* in which a number of these essays have appeared, and to Mary E. Kennan, the Prentice Hall Press editor who suggested this book and shepherded it to publication.

Good friends and companions who have shared the joys of birding with me have had a hand in this effort, providing information, inspiration, and encouragement. Moral support from family members, birders and non-birders, has been most rewarding. It is my good fortune to have a husband who shares my addiction to birds and a son who understands it.

Not the least of my indebtedness is to the generous field trip leaders—volunteers all—who tolerated my ignorance and contributed to my ornithological education. I can never repay them; the best I can do is to pass it on.

Solitary Sandpiper

PART ONE

Thoughts on Birding and Bird Watching

Two Different Species

OUR NEIGHBORS CALL US BIRD WATCHERS, AND ALTHOUGH we don't mind the term, it seems inadequate. It evokes images of armchair nature lovers who sprinkle crumbs on windowsills and sit back to watch the birds that gather to feed.

Not that there's anything wrong with that. Obviously, it brings great satisfaction to thousands of people who never travel beyond their back yards in search of birds. There is much to be said for enjoyment of that which is close at hand, so perhaps we should be content to class ourselves as bird watchers.

But right now we are *birders*, engaging in a more strenuous activity than merely watching birds. We are seekers of birds, going out in all weather and at all hours of day and night to find birds in their natural habitats, knowing that most of them will never come to us.

Wading through swamps, climbing rocky mountain slopes, fighting mosquitoes in summer and frostbite in winter, we endure hardships that would make even a presidential candidate throw in the towel. And all for the glimpse (and often *only* a glimpse) of a bird whose picture we can see in any number of books and whose lifestyle has been recorded in the most intimate detail for the benefit of television viewers who can do their bird watching in safety and comfort.

But this two-dimensional view, even in living color, is only an appetizer for birders. They have to experience it themselves. It is not enough to be observers of the whole nature scene; they must be a part of it. And so they travel to search out the rare and secretive birds, to follow migrations, and to soak up all the atmosphere that the camera cannot capture.

Before they travel, they do their homework. They study the life patterns and behavior of birds—their songs, their range, their feeding habits, their courtship and mating, their nesting, and their migration routes. This leads to a study of geography, of wind, weather, and tides, of environmental changes and shifting bird populations, all of which enhances understanding and appreciation.

So when birders go afield, they usually know what they can expect to find—and they always hope to find the unexpected: the earliest migrant to arrive, the latest to depart, the straggler from a foreign shore, the wanderer from remote regions of our continent.

All these are recorded. Birders are great record keepers. Many of them keep both geographical and chronological records of bird sightings. There are back yard lists, county lists, state lists, North American lists, and world lists; day lists, trip lists, and year lists. And of course all birders have life lists—the record of every bird they have identified in the field in their lifetimes, and when and where they first saw it.

Birders plan their vacations carefully, choosing the place and time of year that will offer the greatest opportunity to add new birds to the life list.

This is an interest that adds an extra dimension to travel—one that is not understood by the non-birder.

Once at a party we met a man from Tucson and started the conversation by commenting on the marvelous variety of birds in his part of the country. Yes, he was aware that there were a lot of birds there, he said, and that people traveled from all over the country to see them. But he couldn't imagine why.

That ended *that* conversation.

A few years ago when I was driving through Florida, I planned my route to go through Clewiston, on Lake Okechobee, famed as "The Home of the Smooth-Billed Ani" (not to be confused with the groove-billed ani, which is found in the Rio Grande Valley). I had studied pictures of this grackle-sized black bird with its heavy, parrot-like beak, and I had familiarized myself with its call by listening to a tape as I drove. I thought it would be easy to find flocks of anis, which were reported to have a roosting place in the trees behind the high school to which they retreated after feeding in adjacent farm fields.

All was quiet around the high school that Saturday morning except for three small boys playing on the basketball court. I stopped and asked them if they had seen a flock of black birds in the vicinity.

"I seen a crow," the biggest boy offered.

I explained the difference between the smooth-billed ani and the crow, played the tape to demonstrate the former's distinctive call, and then showed him the picture in the field guide.

He listened politely, studied the picture, then looked at me with a wary suspicion that is reserved for the demented and asked the obvious question that will forever separate birders from non-birders:

"Whatcha gonna do with him when you find him?"

Such Nice People

A VIENNESE FRIEND OF MINE, INTRIGUED IN A BAFFLED sort of way by Americans who pursue wild birds, once quizzed me at length about a field trip I was anticipating.

"With whom do you go?" she wanted to know. "Are they nice people?" And she bubbled with laughter at my instantaneous reply, "Of course!"

She thought I was touchingly naïve. Her field was medicine, and she admitted freely that even among practitioners of the healing arts, she often encountered men and women with certain undesirable traits, some she would even describe as obnoxious. Did this never happen among birders?

"Rarely," I reflected, not quite willing to go as far as Will Rogers and declare that I'd never met a birder I didn't like. But I suggested to her that if I met some of her obnoxious colleagues on a birding trip, I might find them charming, congenial companions.

Whether birding brings out the best of people or the best *in* people, I couldn't say. It may work both ways.

But I do know that in our years of birding, my husband and I have met many fine people, and our lives have been enriched by the close friendships we have formed with kindred spirits we might never have met but for this shared pursuit.

In my praise of birders, I must admit to a certain bias. I came to the world of birding from the world of politics, and for several years I had a foot in each world, so it was natural for me from the beginning to draw contrasts between my weekday associates and those with whom I shared weekend adventures. They may have been equally fine people, but in the competitive world of politics, there is a strong accent on the ego. So in my weekday environment I was accustomed to the constant cry (roughly translated): "Look at me! Look at me!"

Small wonder that I was impressed when I went out with a group of happily anonymous birders whose sole message was: "Look at the bird!"

Much of the time we did not know one another's names, nor did we inquire about occupation or status in life. The bird was the thing, and we were too intent on the pursuit to engage in personal exchanges.

It would be foolish to imply that birders are utterly lacking in ego, but they do have a healthy perspective of themselves in the total scheme of things. In the field they have countless opportunities to learn humility, so they readily acknowledge fallibility in themselves and forgive it in others.

Birders do not constitute what the politicians call a "single-interest group." They may be intense, but they are not narrow. On the contrary, they are generally characterized by a broad range of interests, not just in nature and the environment but also in literature, the arts, politics, and sports. (They tend to prefer tennis over team sports, but there are some who are devotees of football, baseball, bowling, and soccer.)

In intellectual curiosity they rate higher than average. They are eager learners—and enthusiastic teachers.

They are philosophical in adversity, for they have

learned to accept nature on its own terms. One marvels at the unfailing good humor of men and women who plunge bravely into mosquito-infested swamps and tick-infested fields; who endure tropical heat and arctic cold; who become sick at sea but never sick at heart even when a rugged pelagic trip is exasperatingly unproductive; who splash through rain and slog through mud, who face bitter winds and blinding snow for the sake of a Christmas Count or even the sight of one special rare bird. They may complain when, at a critical moment, their glasses or binoculars steam over and obscure the view of a transitory bird. But on the whole they are an uncommonly good-humored lot.

Most birders have a pleasant sense of humor and can easily direct it on themselves—laughing at their own foibles and fanaticism, at their mishaps and miscalls in the field.

They have a generosity of spirit, for the essence of the birding experience is sharing. They share their sightings, their trip notes, their literature; they share their cars, their lunches, their insect repellent, their Dramamine. In emergencies I have known them to share warm gloves and boots, their spotting scopes, even their binoculars (the ultimate sacrifice) when on a trip with an unprepared novice.

But above all, they share an appreciation that transcends verbal communication.

There is a special bond between people who have stood together at dawn listening to the calls of willets echoing over a salt marsh, or at dusk watching the nuptial flight of the woodcock; who have walked together out over windswept beaches to follow the flight of gannets over the crests of the waves; who have shared the sight of the first flock of snow geese in autumn and the first warbler in spring.

Such experiences as these are not forgotten, nor are the companions who shared them.

Nice people? Of course!

Getting Hooked on Birds

THE ICE-BREAKER QUESTION WHEN BIRDERS GET TOGETHER is: "How long have you been birding?" The follow-up is: "How did you get hooked?"

A lucky few who started young may kill the conversation by answering to the first question: "All my life." But most of us went into our birding phase in our mature years and, like recent converts, are eager to talk about it. We remember vividly the magic moment and the magic bird that changed our way of life.

For one of our birding companions, the magic moment came one day when she was standing alone on a beach, looking at a resting flock of shorebirds. She savored the beauty of the tranquil scene, but suddenly she realized that there were several different kinds of birds congregated—and she didn't know the name of a single one of them! She made haste to overcome her ignorance and has become an outstanding authority on birds—especially shorebirds, her first love.

For me, the magic moment came on the first of May in 1969. The magic bird was a prothonotary warbler.

Prothonotary Warbler

A few days earlier my husband had come home, quite pleased with himself, and announced, "I enrolled us in the Audubon Society today."

He got a ho-hum reaction. "I thought we were already members," I said, pointing to the latest *Audubon* magazine on the coffee table.

"That's National," he explained patiently. "I joined the local Audubon Society—the one that has the bookstore in Georgetown. They have all kinds of programs and field trips. I thought you'd like that."

Of course I would like it. But I didn't think *he* would. We had grown up quite differently: he in the city, playing tennis in public parks and unaware of any birds except pigeons and robins; I in the country, rambling through woods and over farm fields, making notes of the birds I saw, identified to the best of my ability without aid of binoculars, but with the help of the handy Chester Reed field guide.

I left all that behind for the serious business of getting an education and launching a career and a family. I had never been on an organized bird walk in my life.

But here was my city-bred husband, all enthusiastic over the Society's calendar of field trips he had brought home. How could this be? The answer was simple enough. Ted is a purposeful man, highly resistant to exercise-for-exercise's-sake, one who always found excuses when I suggested going for a walk. But he said that he would be glad to go for walks to look at birds.

In our innocence, neither of us knew that bird watching is a questionable form of exercise, requiring more standing then walking. Nor did we realize that we were embarking on a program that was to change our whole way of life.

When we signed up for our first weekend bird walk, no one warned us that it could be habit forming.

Among the group of fifteen or so, we were clearly the only novices. Our leader that bright, crisp May morning was Sarah Baker, and we learned more about birds and birding from her in the following four hours than either of us had learned in all our previous years of existence.

We learned how to dress. The thought of wearing gloves in May had never occurred to us, but Sarah pointed out that she always carried gloves in her pocket, knowing how chilly it can be along the Potomac in the early hours of morning, even in May.

We learned how to use our inexpensive binoculars and our newly purchased field guide.

We learned the etiquette of the trail, the importance of moving quietly and talking softly. We learned to use our ears as well as our eyes for locating birds. We learned how to follow directions to a bird in a tree. And we learned that "eleven o'clock in the sycamore" is meaningful only to those who can differentiate between a sycamore and an elm.

We learned that there was a staggering fund of information yet to be mastered.

But above all we learned what we had been missing all those years. It was appalling to think of those wasted years.

That day, in four hours, we saw sixty-five species of birds. We will never forget that number: sixty-five different birds, and most of them completely new and unheard of, as far as we were concerned. Most of them were warblers (that did not warble but buzzed or chipped or trilled). They had fascinating names: black-throated blue, black-throated green, parula (Sarah taught us its buzzy trill that went up the scale and snapped off in a staccato note at the end). There were chestnut-sided warblers, bay-breasted warblers, prairie and Canada warblers.

When we discovered the little black-masked yellowthroat, I felt a special delight. Here was an old friend in the midst of all these strangers; it alone, among all the warblers, was a familiar sight from my midwest childhood. When I heard its "Witchety-witchety-witch" song, I did not need to be told its name.

But the bird of the day was the prothonotary warbler. Sarah had told us that we would see one, but I was dubious. I had heard of the fabled prothonotary. I had read all about it in the accounts of the Alger Hiss trial, back in the 1940s, and I had gathered from the testimony given by Whittaker Chambers and some United States senator who fancied himself a great bird watcher that the prothonotary warbler Alger Hiss had seen was a very rare bird, one that I would not see during years of searching.

But Sarah Baker led us straight to it. A turn in the path and suddenly there we were, eyeball to eyeball with that incredible golden bird. He looked us over, threw back his head, and serenaded us (and presumably some listening female prothonotary) with his ringing, uninhibited song.

That was the magic moment, the turning point. We might have ended that first walk feeling frustrated over the fleeting glimpses of all the other warblers, but after that leisurely, close-up encounter with the prothonotary, we were hooked, and our lives would never be the same.

Unexpected Rewards

WE ARE NIGHT PEOPLE, MY HUSBAND AND I, SLOW TO
awake in the morning, dreamy-eyed until after the second cup of coffee, and not fully functioning until about
four o'clock in the afternoon.

Or rather, that's the way we were in our pre-birding
life.

Now, it is not at all unthinkable to arise at four in the
morning in order to be at a favorite birding spot at dawn.
We can even forgo the morning cup of coffee in favor
of an earlier start. The lure of migration is a stronger
stimulant than caffeine, and we know of many people
whose addiciton to nicotine has been replaced by the
more benign addiction of birding. Even those who continue to smoke rarely do so in the field. It is just too
complicated to manage cigarettes and binoculars at the
same time. Moreover, the activity is so absorbing that
often the cigarette compulsion is forgotten.

Nor are birders given to imbibing strong spirits in
excess. They want to be alert and well coordinated in

the field, and if they are to be up and doing at dawn, they can ill afford late-night imbibing and early-morning tremors. Birding is a healthful activity, and even if it does not provide the best form of exercise, it does at least take you out into the fresh air and sunshine and away from the centers of pollution. We know of more than one recovering coronary patient who has found it the ideal activity, both for physical and mental health.

After a day in the field, trivia and minor irritations seem to melt away. Major problems become less burdensome, seen in a new perspective. And families who have suffered incomprehensible tragedy have found solace in the world of nature. A couple we have encountered on the trail took up birding after the suicide of their only child—a bright, promising young man who had shown none of the warning symptoms. There was no answer to the haunting question, "Why?" There was no relief from the bereft parents' grief—until a friend took them on a bird walk, and gradually they found the peace that had eluded them since their son's death.

Another couple, coping with the heart-breaking problem of teenage drug abuse in the family, preserved their sanity by taking long walks, just to get out of the house. On their walks, they discovered birds—and a new way of life opened up to them.

Again and again we have observed that couples who bird together tend to stay together. I can think of few things that are more conducive to marital harmony than sharing the joys and excitement of discovering new birds and learning their songs, of witnessing a mass migration in the fall and welcoming the returning birds in the spring.

Birding sharpens perception, heightens awareness of the world around us in all its beauty and variety, deepens aesthetic appreciation. It can, at the same time, calm and excite the senses.

The lure of birds can turn stay-at-homes into bold adventurers, eager to explore new territories where birds

may be found. Forsaking the sedentary life, they grav-
itate toward out-of-the-way spots that they would never
have discovered otherwise, and in the process they learn
more about the countryside and its geography. Those
who resisted map study begin to hoard maps of all kinds,
including the mysterious topographic maps that never
seemed to make sense.

Weather maps, too, become subjects of intense interest. Birders develop a new awareness of weather patterns, not merely out of concern for their own comfort
in the field, but with the knowledge that the movement
of birds is affected by the movement of weather systems.
They watch for winds that will give migration a push
or hold it back. They study the trends that produce good
hawk flights in the fall, and after a coastal storm, they
watch for reports of rare birds blown off course.

One of the greatest benefits of joining the birding
fraternity is the camaraderie enjoyed by people who
share the same interests and values. Two birders meeting as strangers on the trail soon become involved in
animated conversation, and such a chance encounter
may lead to a life-long friendship. Age differences are
of no consequence in this fraternity. A keen youngster
of eight or nine can be just as comfortable on a field trip
as an octogenarian; in fact, they will find much in common, and both will be unmindful of the so-called generation gap. Lucky is the young person who becomes
interested in the pursuit of birds early in life and can
look forward to a whole lifetime of rewarding adventures.

Those adventures may lead to distant shores or merely
into the next county. And they may lead to a whole
world of wonders, of which birds are only a small part,
a mere introduction.

"Knowing how way leads on to way," as Robert Frost
wrote in his poem "The Road Not Taken." It is not
surprising that a person who goes out to watch birds
will begin to develop an interest in trees, for it is often
desirable to be able to identify the tree in which a bird

is perched. Is it an oak or an elm, a birch or a sycamore? It soon becomes apparent that certain birds prefer certain trees for food supply or nesting sites. Shrubs, too, fall under closer scrutiny.

From trees and shrubs, the birder may move on to a study of ferns and wildflowers, or reptiles and mammals, spiders and insects. The ecology of a swamp and the erosion of a shoreline may become matters of great interest to someone who, in pre-birding days, never gave them a passing thought.

Interest in birds inevitably leads to an interest in the total habitat and food supply. Concern with the health of the environment becomes a global concern to those who follow the migration of birds. They begin to comprehend that what happens to the rain forests of Costa Rica has a direct effect on their favorite birds, the birds that brighten their summers and then leave in the fall for a warmer climate.

Birding broadens our horizons and enriches our lives. And happily, it is habit forming.

The Hazards of Birding

MOST PEOPLE THINK OF BIRD WATCHING AS A NICE, SAFE, comfortable activity. But those who engage in it know its minor discomforts and its major hazards. They endure insect bites in summer and risk frostbite in winter. They learn to be wary of ticks and snakes and of birding while driving.

They have heard tales of traffic accidents involving several cars in a caravan of birders when the lead car came to a sudden stop, and they know how quickly a lone driver can swerve on a fast interstate highway when he or she catches sight of an interesting bird.

They have had constant reminders of teacherous footing in slimy bogs and on rocky mountain slopes. We know one veteran birder who suffered a broken jaw and extensive dental damage at a hawk-watch station when he placed his foot and his trust on an unreliable rock.

There are more subtle hazards, too, as we discovered the year we moved to Melody Lane. The memory greens with every spring.

Moving a household is a traumatic experience for any family, at any time. But it is cruel and unjust punishment for a family of birders to have to accomplish a move in the middle of spring migration.

The timing could not have been worse. Just when we should have been free to follow the birds from dawn to dark, we were sentenced to days and nights of hard labor, packing and unpacking, cleaning floors, washing windows, and all the other unrewarding chores that fate had dumped upon us.

At last, on an irresistibly lovely day in May, we called time out. Leaving the packing crates behind, we took to the woods and fields, burdened by nothing more than binoculars, field guides, insect repellent, and lunch. It was a glorious, carefree feeling, and we were relieved to find that the migration had not completely passed us by.

That night we fell into bed with all the satisfying visions of a day well spent: of osprey carrying shining fish in their talons; of swallows swooping over a placid pond; of green herons stalking a meal at the water's edge; of vultures soaring over fields; of orioles flitting through sycamore branches; and of warblers darting through the trees.

They were all there: the black-throated blues and black-throated greens; bright magnolias and plain Tennessees; zebra-striped black-and-whites; soft-blue ceruleans; parulas already engaged in nest building; and brilliant yellow prothonotaries, their heads thrown back in exuberant song.

The next night, after a day of devotion to household chores, the visions were entirely different.

At bedtime, I looked down and saw beside my slippers a cream-colored movement on the cream-colored carpet we had inherited from the former owners of our new home. An unpleasant-looking little grub was emerging from the thick pile.

With my attention now focused on the floor that I had

vacuumed thoroughly only two days earlier, I saw another . . . and another . . . and another. In the next half-hour we harvested nearly 200 wriggling little bodies, mainly in the bedroom, but some in the hall and on the carpeted stairs. And the next hour was spent searching, first *for* the books, then *through* the books that would help us identify the little creatures.

We unpacked the microscope and had a closer look at the enemy but went to bed at last, in the early hours of morning, with the mystery unsolved. Our uneasy sleep was filled with dreams of larvae crawling out of the walls and woodwork.

By dawn's early light, we found more of them struggling to the surface of the carpet, and we wondered what horrible kind of infestation we had unwittingly acquired along with our dream house.

The Department of Agriculture, we felt, could certainly help us. The entomologist who viewed the specimen was baffled. It was clearly a larva, but one he could not immediately identify. Definitely it was not that of a carpet moth or beetle, or any of the usual household pests. He would have to study it and call us.

Twenty-four anxious hours passed before we heard from him again. I suspect the delay was due more to embarrassment than to prolonged research. The larva, he admitted, was one he should have recognized at once. It belonged to the common house fly.

The news brought a great sense of relief but left us mystified. Why so many? How did they get there?

Clever deduction produced the answer. The larvae were souvenirs of our idyllic day afield. Somewhere, one of us (probably I) had picked up a nearly-ripe egg sac and brought it safely home in the tread of a boot—just in time for it to hatch on our bedroom carpet.

We now had a new rule to add to our list of birder precautions (always carry insect repellent; de-tick after spring and summer forays; check the rear-view mirror before you brake; etc.). This was a lesson we could have learned from Kipling's cave woman, who sprinkled clean sand on the floor of the cave and instructed her mate when he came home from the hunt: "Wipe your feet, dear, before you come in, and we'll keep house."

PART TWO

Blessed Are the Beginners

Beginners Are Welcome

THE VOICE ON THE PHONE SOUNDED YOUNG AND EAGER. Was it too late to sign up for tomorrow's bird walk?

I assured her that it was not and gave her directions to the rendezvous point.

There was a pause and then she said, almost apologetically, "I've never been on a bird walk before, but it just seems like such nice weather to be out. . . ."

It was, indeed, perfect spring weather, too perfect to stay indoors. I encouraged her to come. Still she sounded hesitant.

"I don't—" she began. "I mean—do you have to *know* anything to go on these walks?"

"Just one thing," I told her. "It's going to be ten degrees colder than you expect, so wear one more layer than you think you'll need."

She confessed that she didn't own binoculars. That was no problem; I promised to bring a spare, and I hung up wondering why so many newcomers to birding feel compelled to apologize for their ignorance. If they only realized what an asset they are on a field trip! Coming fresh, with enthusiasm to share, they form a fine symbiotic relationship with the experienced birders who have knowledge to share and are eager to share it.

I remembered myself as a novice on the birding trail, awed by the vast store of information the leaders had at their command, overwhelmed when I contemplated the depths of my ignorance. And I recalled how kind everyone was—kind, and at times almost envious. One of my leaders expressed that envy when I asked, in my usual apologetic manner, for information about the fall trip to Cape May, New Jersey, to watch the migration.

"Is this your first trip?" he asked, though he had to know how green I was. And when I admitted to it, I saw the nostalgic glint in his eye.

"I wish it were *my* first," he said.

Now, years later, I know so well what he was feeling. We all cherish our "firsts," and through the eyes of beginners we experience them all over again.

I would have to explain that to my hesitant caller— if she showed up. I still had my doubts and would not have been surprised if she had backed out at the last minute.

But she did show up, along with a dozen birders with varying degrees of experience, and she stole the show, not with her expertise but with her unrestrained enthusiasm and delight at each new discovery.

She adapted quickly to binoculars, with little of the frustration that is normal to beginners, and even with the naked eye she was quick to spot birds that others might have missed. She didn't know what she was seeing, but her descriptions were like quick bird-identification quizzes for the whole group.

Her "raspberry-colored sparrow" was clearly a purple finch. Her "gray little bird with a crest" was a tufted titmouse. When she caught sight of a "beautiful little blue-and-black-and-white bird," everyone leaped to attention, ready to focus on a black-throated blue warbler, until our beginner gasped in astonishment, "Oh, look! He's walking upside down!" And then we knew she was watching a white-breasted nuthatch as it worked its way, head-first, down a treetrunk. Its blue-gray back looked more blue than gray to her. But that was before she saw the bluebirds.

Someone else spotted them first, a pair of them, in a low branch overhanging the trail. By that time everyone in the group was bent upon making sure that the new-comer got a good look at every bird that was sighted, for to her every bird was a life bird, with the possible exception of the cardinals and crows. So everyone pushed her to the front, telling her exactly where to look, waiting expectantly for the reaction of a young woman who had never seen bluebirds before.

She did not see them at once. Then suddenly the male dropped to the path just ahead of us, his blue wings flashing in the sunlight. She saw it—and we saw it through her eyes, as if we were seeing a bluebird our-selves for the first time.

"Oh, that color!" she exclaimed softly. "I've never *seen* such a blue before!"

While she stood, entranced, with her binoculars fixed on the bright-hued male on the ground, his subtler-hued mate dropped down beside him and posed nicely for comparison. Then suddenly a whole family of bluebirds materialized from nowhere, and there were six of them feeding on the ground only a few yards away.

Our beginner was speechless.

We could have stayed there all morning watching the bluebirds display their incredible colors, but there were more birds to be found. We moved on, and the thought occurred to me that everything would be anticlimactic after that show. But we had not yet seen a northern oriole. Or a scarlet tanager. Or a redstart. Or a yellow warbler.

We saw all of those and more. And in the process of locating them for our new recruit, we sharpened our own observations of field marks and behavior. Our field guides were opened more frequently than usual; we took time for closer study of each bird, even the familiar ones.

Common grackles took on an uncommon beauty; red-winged blackbirds looked wonderfully exotic. There was a newness to everything that bright spring morning because we were seeing it in what G. K. Chesterton called "the sunlight of surprise."

Our beginner had made a good trip a very special trip, and I regretted that I did not get a chance to explain this to her. But maybe it wasn't necessary. On parting, when she expressed her thanks to everyone for being

Nuthatch

so helpful and tolerant, she was answered by a spon-
taneous chorus: "Thank *you* for joining us." And she
must have caught that same nostalgic glint that I had
seen in the eyes of the old hand who took time, years
ago, to tell me all about the migration at Cape May.

Birding by Ear

THE LITTLE GIRL NEXT DOOR, WHO HAD LEARNED SOME-
thing about birds in her second grade nature study class,
brought us the report of a great horned owl in her backyard. I was impressed.

"Did you see it?" I asked.

"Not yet," she replied confidently. "But I've heard it.
It says, 'Whoooo, whooo.' "

What the bird was really saying, I suspected, was
"Cooo, cooo." Birds have a way of saying different things
to different people, and mourning doves that say, "Cooo,
cooo" to Roger Tory Peterson (and me) may very well
say, "Whooo, whooo" to a budding young bird watcher
intent on finding a great horned owl.

Translating bird calls into English is a risky practice
and one that can lead to endless arguments. Does the
white-throated sparrow really say, "Poor Sam Peabody,
Peabody, Peabody"? Or is he saying, as some claim,
"Oh, sweet Canada, Canada, Canada"? Whichever it
is, it is not a totally reliable identification of the unseen

bird, for he often sings an incomplete song. Early in the spring, when he starts loosening up his chilled vocal cords, it may be only two notes, high and thin, terminating abruptly, as if he has forgotten the rest—or hasn't yet learned it. Still, the experienced ear will recognize it for its *quality* rather than its message.

The same is true of the Carolina wren, which has a variety of songs but is easy to recognize, regardless of variations, by the clear, ringing quality of his voice and the incredible volume in proportion to his size. My husband says there should be a special award to the Carolina wren for producing the highest decibel output per cubic centimeter of bird.

The best way to become familiar with his repertoire and vocal quality is by listening to him in the field. The next best way is to listen to a recording. Either way is preferable to relying on verbal descriptions. This is obvious from the controversies that arise over the Carolina wren's familiar two-syllable song, repeated three times.

Peterson translates it as "Wheedle, wheedle, wheedle." I have a friend who insists it is "Tricky, tricky, tricky," and another friend who thinks it is "Turkey, turkey, turkey." To me, it sounds more like "Gertie, Gertie, Gertie!" As for his three-syllable song, I can't imagine where anyone got the idea he was singing about a teakettle. To me, it's very clear that he's calling for "Cheeseburger, cheeseburger, cheeseburger!"

In my early searches for the ovenbird, I was thrown off course many times by the description of his call as "Teacher, teacher, teacher." There were dozens of birds saying "Teacher" to me, including the Carolina wren and the tufted titmouse. (My mother called the titmouse "the preacher bird"; *she* thought it was saying, "Preacher, preacher, preacher.") But the consensus seems to be that he is calling his own name over and over—or that of a lost brother: "Peter, Peter, Peter."

Many birds do announce their own names: the killdeer, the chickadee, the veery, the jay, and supposedly the towhee, although he slurs over the first syllable so rapidly it sounds more to me like a simple, "Shreik!" And a serious-minded beginner once asked, in response to the information that the phoebe gives its own name: "Can birds actually reproduce that 'f' sound?"

There are more complex songs that can only be translated into full sentences. A neighbor of ours had a resident northern (Baltimore) oriole that, she alleged, watched her at work in the potato patch and sang out, "Didn't find any potato bugs, did you?"

I doubted that. I didn't think the oriole was even speaking English. Not all birds do. The magnolia warbler, for one, speaks in classic Latin. When he arrives in my backyard in the spring, he announces, like Julius Caesar: "Veni, vidi, vici."

As for my little friend's great horned owl, did I tell her that she was hearing nothing more exotic than the fat, lazy dove that sits on my feeder in plain sight every day? Certainly not. She'll discover that for herself soon enough. In the meantime, let her continue her happy search for the big owl she expects to find lurking in the woods. The search is the thing, as all birders know.

What's in a Name?

My neighbor lured me across the street one day last summer with the intriguing report of "yellow-breasted sparrows" nesting on her carport.

The nest was neatly plastered against an exposed beam, just under the ceiling, and supported by an abandoned wasp nest. Although there were no birds on the nest at the moment, its construction identified the builders immediately.

"They're barn swallows," I told her, but she brushed this piece of information off as purely personal opinion.

"Oh, is that what *you* call them? *I* call them yellow-breasted sparrows."

One name, apparently, is just as good as any other.

There is no point in arguing with people who choose to name birds for themselves. I learned that long ago on a visit to my sister's farm. One morning her husband called us to the window to see the "whole flock of little orioles" on the driveway. Since he was farm bred and was generally knowledgeable about wildlife, I assumed he knew what he was talking about and rushed to see the phenomenon. Even in migration season I had never witnessed a "whole flock" of orioles of any kind.

The sight turned out to be something less than phenomenal.

"They're goldfinches!" I exclaimed, in ill-concealed disappointment, as the flock exploded into the air.

If my brother-in-law was unaffected by my lack of diplomacy, he was equally unimpressed by my identification. His reply was tolerant, even slightly amused.

"Is that what *you* call them? *I* call them little orioles."

And he still does.

If he had called them "wild canaries," it would not have bothered me. That was the affectionate name local people gave the American goldfinch when I was a child, and I accepted that as I accepted the apt nickname of "butcher-bird" for the loggerhead shrike that impaled grasshoppers on barbed wire to dissect them. But I had been taught at an early age that proper names are essential to communication, and accuracy takes precedence over whim.

I was seven years old when I first encountered the word *starling* in an English story. What a lovely, musical name for a bird! Blissfully ignorant of the real starlings, which had not yet flocked across the midwest, I promptly applied the name to our red-winged blackbirds. These beautiful birds certainly deserved something better than to be categorized with the detested "blackbirds" that created such a din and mess in the schoolyard each fall.

My father, reviewing my list of bird sightings, corrected me on the starling and told me that, like it or not, "red-winged blackbird" was the proper name, not a local nickname, and that the imported European starling, a quite different species, was found only in the eastern states.

Regretfully, I corrected my list. Where my father got his information I did not know, but I did not question his authority. His eyes and ears were always alert to birdlife as he roamed the Illinois farmland. Without benefit of binoculars or field guide, he was quick to identify every species of duck in flight along the Mississippi Flyway, and he recognized cuckoos and meadowlarks as readily as the quail and pheasants that provided fare for our table.

He also spoke familiarly of exotic species I never saw in my wanderings: mud-hens and hell-divers and fly-up-the-creeks.

It was years before I learned that his mud-hens were American coots; his ominous-sounding hell-divers were innocent little pied-billed grebes; and his fly-up-the-creek was the elusive green-backed heron. All these were colloquial names, generally accepted by local hunters and farmers who never knew the proper names.

I was delighted to discover them all, in recent years, as "Other Names" in Edward Howe Forbush's *Natural History of American Birds of Eastern and Central North America*. That discovery helped to restore confidence in my original authority. It was a relief to know that my father, who had set me straight on starlings, had not been guilty himself of assigning names to birds to suit his caprice.

When I shared my information with him, he was pleased to learn the correct names of these old familiar friends and to study their pictures in my *Birds of North America*.

I forgot to ask him where he ever got the name of "titlark" for the bird I later came to know as the dickcissel. I can find no source for the name. But no matter. By now I am beyond the stage of relying on parental infallibility—or on local observers with no expertise in the field.

The Well-Dressed Birder

SHE WAS A COLOR-COORDINATED VISION IN CERISE PANTS, pink blouse, and lilac sweater. Her blonde hair was tied back prettily in a chiffon scarf that matched her blouse and her lipstick.

When we all introduced ourselves at the parking-lot rendezvous she gave her name and added rather shyly, and unnecessarily: "This is my first bird walk."

We knew. And we were afraid it would be her last. Her "walking shoes" were designed for walking paved city blocks, and it was doubtful that she would be able to finish the course over the rugged terrain.

We welcomed her, as birders always welcome newcomers, and tried conscientiously to put her at ease, realizing how she must be reacting to this raggle-taggle lot she was joining. There was no doubt that we all felt a little of the smug superiority of the old hands who had learned long ago exactly what was meant by the trip instructions to "dress warmly" and "wear comfortable shoes."

Yet our smugness was diluted by a tinge of self-consciousness in the presence of this impeccably dressed young woman, even though we knew that her lovely lilac sweater would soon be snagged and her polished shoes muddy and scuffed. There was that brief moment of seeing ourselves as others saw us: unkempt, unpolished, and unpressed. And as we set out on the trail, I heard some rare apologetic remarks.

A white-haired lady wearing baggy dungarees and several layers of shirts topped by an ancient Army jacket murmured something about its shabby appearance.

"It was my brother's," she explained to a middle-aged birder walking beside her, "from the first World War, of course. I've always loved it. But I really should throw it away, I suppose."

"Oh, no!" her hiking companion demurred in shocked tones. "One should never throw away a garment that is serviceable!"

A non-birder friend once observed, half in envy, "Birders don't care what they wear." That isn't true. Birders do care what they wear; they just don't care much how they look, as long as they're comfortable. In the field, the bird's the thing—and there is little time to observe what fellow birders are wearing.

But at lunch breaks and in leisure moments, they often discuss clothing—from the standpoint of function, not fashion.

"How do you like your Bean boots? Do they keep your feet warm? How many socks do you wear with them?"

"Where did you get your jacket? I need one like that—with pockets big enough for a bird guide."

"Are those gloves waterproof? Mine are fine until I get caught in the rain or a wet snow."

Birders are always eager to learn what holds up best, what keeps them comfortable in the field, in fair weather and foul. They generally choose somber, inconspicuous colors, although there may be an occasional down jacket of bright red or royal blue. But always the main criterion is comfort.

The "layered look" was discovered by birders long before the fashion world picked it up. Starting out early in the morning and staying out all day, they have to adjust to a range of temperatures from pre-dawn chill to midday heat, and so they deck themselves out in layers that are easily peeled off along the way. They like lightweight jackets that can be stowed away in a knapsack or tied around the waist as the day warms up.

Even in hot weather, they prefer to have arms and legs covered to protect them from insect bites and bramble scratches.

Pockets are important for carrying car keys, gloves, bird guides, notebooks, insect repellent, and emergency rations.

Some brave souls bare their heads to sun, wind, and insect pests, but most choose to wear a hat—usually a disreputable model that can be stuffed into a pocket when not in use. It must be lightweight so that it doesn't rest too heavily on the skull in the summer heat; short of brim, so as not to interfere with binoculars; and a firm enough fit to withstand capricious breezes.

Footgear is the subject of much birder discussion. Some insist on hiking shoes or waterproof boots; others settle for sneakers in warm weather, reconciling themselves to getting their feet wet now and then. Sneakers are lightweight and inexpensive—and they do dry quickly after a dunking.

Raingear, too, is carefully chosen. There are wetboots and wetsuits, ponchos and rain-resistant parkas. I have even seen birders with umbrellas, which are admittedly awkward to handle, but they have the advantage of keeping binoculars and eyeglasses dry in a downpour.

A birder's winter wardrobe includes thermal underwear, wool and cotton socks, boots with liners, wool gloves and lined leather gloves, a variety of shirts of different weights and fabrics, sleeveless sweaters and vests, cardigans, mufflers, heavy jeans and warm-up pants, down jackets, and a choice of headgear, ranging from fleece-lined hoods to knitted caps and ski masks, which are essential for protecting the face against wind chill, especially on a coastal or pelagic trip.

Well-padded and thoroughly disguised, winter birders set out with their pockets bulging with spare gloves, ear muffs, battery-operated hand warmers, and plenty of tissues for drippy noses and steamed-over lenses. With nothing but eyes and nose tips showing, they have difficulty recognizing one another—but the important thing is to recognize the bird, not the birders.

I never saw the lady in the lilac sweater again—at least not in the lilac sweater. I remember the color especially because her lips were a matching shade at the end of that brisk April morning walk. But she finished the trip without complaint, thanked our leader through chattering teeth, and dived into her car.

She could have been one of the fast learners. Who knows? I may have seen her on the trail many times since, disguised beyond recognition in drab and shapeless garb carefully chosen for function and—what was the old timer's word?—serviceability. She may even be wearing an old Army jacket handed down to her by her father—from World War II, of course.

Checklists, Life Lists, and the Bird du Jour

WHEN WE WERE BEGINNING BIRDERS, WE CARRIED CHECK-lists with us on field trips and spent more time writing down the names of the birds that other people saw than we did observing the birds ourselves. It was a typical beginner's mistake.

Now we leave our checklists at home. Not that we don't keep records; we do. But now we fill in the checklist from memory when we get home. Over coffee or lunch (often a very late lunch, because a birder in the field never knows what time it is), we settle down for the ritual of the tally.

By this time the order of the checklist is well fixed in our minds so that we no longer complain (as many beginners do) that "it isn't even in alphabetical order." It is in a more logical order—the same order as that followed by the field guides, which, as Chandler Robbins explains in his introduction to *Birds of North America*, is a ' "natural' or evolutionary order, progressing from the least to the more advanced families of birds."

Wouldn't it destroy all sense of family to group rails, ravens, redstarts, roadrunners, and robins all together, merely for the sake of alphabetical convenience? It is much more comfortable to know that birds that flock together in the field also flock together on the checklist: herons and egrets; ducks and geese; chickadees and titmice; grackles and cowbirds.

Checking them off on the list is like taking the daily attendance at school, calling attention not only to those that are present but also to those that are absent. (Where were the bluebirds today? What has happened to the towhees? Are the tree swallows late this year?)

Our totals may range from twenty (on a poor day) to seventy or eighty during spring or fall migration, and since in most seasons we can see as many as twenty species without leaving our own property, anything less than that on a field trip is disappointing.

But numbers are not as significant as quality—quality of the birds seen, and quality of the view. There is some snob value in scarcity, and if we were claiming points for birds, the system would undoubtedly offer extra points for such rarities as peregrine falcons, black rails, or mourning warblers. These all belong in the "Better Bird Department."

But there are also better views of old, familiar birds. I have seen many magnolia warblers in my life, but it was only last summer that I got a close enough look at a magnolia warbler to discover the small yellow patch back of the black face mask. That's where familiarity begins.

Of course we keep life lists, and a life bird on the day's checklist is a major event these days, compared with the early days, when we could go out and add a dozen life birds in one day. And we keep year lists, checking off each species as it appears in its own season and comparing this year's tallies with those of previous years.

But we also keep impressions—visual memories of

new birds seen, or of familiar birds seen in new light. So as we recap the day's experiences and recall the visual images that made the day outstanding, each of us nominates a "Bird of the Day." We call it the Bird *du Jour* Award.

The Bird *du Jour* is not necessarily a new bird; most often it is not. It is a bird seen at unusually close range, engaged in an unusual activity, or in an unusual setting. These are the pictures that stay in the memory and are replayed automatically whenever the name of the bird is mentioned.

Cattle Egret

There is the ruby-crowned kinglet that we saw prac-tically at our feet, at a stop on the Chesapeake Bay Bridge-Tunnel, as he picked up a moth at the edge of the park-ing area and flashed his crimson crown-stripe. There is the cattle egret we surprised in the act of gulping down a frog that was too big to go down comfortably. There is the black-bellied whistling duck sitting on top of a giant yucca in bold silhouette against the sky.

These were not life birds, but they provided life pictures.

If I were awarding a grand prize, it would go to the osprey for his starring role in a performance we caught in Maryland several years ago. We had gone to Hughes Hollow to look for him; it was April, and time for him to appear.

At noon we gave up. As we got in the car to drive away, suddenly there he was, just in from a long flight, and hungry. He hovered in one spot over the pond for a full minute, beating his wings as if treading water, then plunged fifty feet down to capture a fish.

With the red carp in his talons, he winged purpose-fully to a dead tree, and there he settled down to savor his meal—and we settled down to watch through our binoculars at a distance of thirty yards as he tore the fish apart, scale by scale, bone by bone.

It took him forty-eight minutes to finish it off, and for forty-eight minutes we scarcely moved. There could be no question that this was to be our unanimous choice for Bird *du Jour*.

The Birder's Bookshelf

THERE ARE LONELY PEOPLE, I'VE HEARD, WHOSE DAYS ARE spent waiting for the telephone to ring.

There are others whose telephones ring constantly. It is my opinion that this latter group should share the wealth, reveal the secrets of their popularity.

In that spirit—and with no intent to discourage the telephone calls that come as welcome and often entertaining interruptions of my daily routine—I offer this advice to lonely hearts: Set yourself up as a source of instant information on birds, and the world will keep your telephone line busy.

You will need, of course, a genuine interest in birds and in people, not bad attributes to cultivate. Next, you will need a referral system. The local Audubon Society is sure to welcome able volunteers who can be available at their home phones to answer bird questions. Thanks to my own Audubon connection, rarely a day goes by without some intriguing query or pleasantly rewarding conversation.

The third prerequisite is a modest library.

With a shelf of the right reference books adjacent to the telephone, you can amaze your callers with your wisdom and expertise. You need not tell them that you are finding all the answers in the books at your fingertips, or that they could avoid making these phone calls by buying (and studying) a few basic books for themselves. Let them think you're a living encyclopedia—and they will call again and again.

In my years on the telephone network, I've found that these are the books I refer to most frequently:

First are the field guides, for the most common question is: "What was this strange bird I saw?" Since Roger Tory Peterson produced his first edition back in the 1930s, to the eternal gratitude of field birders, other guides have been published, and Peterson's own guide has been revised and expanded in what is commonly known as "the new Peterson." Addicted to books as I am to birds, I buy them all, but the ones I refer to most frequently are Chandler Robbins' *Birds of North America*, The National Geographic *Field Guide to the Birds of North America*, and of course the new Peterson. Each has its unique advantages and disadvantages, and sometimes it is necessary to refer to all three, and others, as I try to match the caller's often-inept description to a picture when the identity does not immediately come to mind.

The bird is seldom a strange one. (I do keep *Birds of Europe* and *Birds of Mexico* on the lower shelf, in the hope of some day identifying a real rarity, but except for a couple of escaped cage birds, this has never happened.) It is more likely to be the description, conjured up by a novice, that is strange. So the pictures in the field guides can offer clues to what the caller is trying to describe.

In some instances, of course, you have to rely on your experience and a lively imagination. "That woodpecker that dives into the water" is obviously not a woodpecker at all but a kingfisher. The "big black bird with a red crest and racing stripes running down its neck" is unmistakably a pileated woodpecker. The "brown bird with a long sharp beak and a body like a football" turns out, surprisingly, to be an American bittern. You might leaf through several field guides before coming up with *that* answer.

The field guides are also important sources of information on habitat, distribution, migration routes, behavior, and songs.

Alongside the field guides is a resource, not a book, that often proves useful when people try to identify a bird by its song. Some are able to give recognizable imitations; others try the impossible task of giving verbal descriptions of a melody or call note. Usually I can hazard a fair guess and then verify it by reaching for the appropriate cassette from *The Field Guide to Bird Song* and playing it over the phone.

It is also useful to know what birds are likely to occur in a given area at a given time of year. In Maryland, we are fortunate to have the small (pocket-size) booklet (popularly called the Yellow Book) titled *Field List of Birds of Maryland*. This "checklist," compiled by Chandler Robbins and Danny Bystrak, is much more than the title implies. In addition to data on all species that have ever been reported in Maryland (including such extinct species as the passenger pigeon, last seen in 1903, and the Carolina parakeet, 1865), it presents in bar-graph form a wealth of information on current Maryland birds: part-time residents, full-time residents, and migrants. At a glance, you can find the nesting dates and habitat for any of the breeding species, the arrival and departure dates of part-time residents and migrants, and the periods of peak abundance.

That's not all. At the back of the booklet is a handy list of "Choice Birding Areas" and their locations and their specialites. This is especially useful in answering such questions as "Where can I go to find a Bewick's wren?"

Even more useful in that respect is Claudia Wilds' *Finding Birds in the National Capital Area*. I reach for it again and again to answer those "Where can I go . . ." and "What's the best place for . . ." questions that are most frequently asked by out-of-town birders visiting the Washington area. It would be better if they bought the book themselves, for it is a pure delight to read it and a pleasure to follow its clear-cut directions, down to the last tenth of a mile, and detailed maps to good birding spots, from the mountains of western Maryland to the Outer Banks of North Carolina. With specific seasonal information, it tells you not only where to go, but when to go in quest of various species.

Next to this paperback volume is the bulkier hardcover *Guide to the National Wildlife Refuges*, by Laura and William Riley, which is used occasionally to give helpful advice to local birders who are planning trips to more remote spots in the United States.

Most of the questions from back yard feeder watchers could be answered by referring to a small, inexpensive booklet, *Attracting Birds in the Piedmont*, edited by Joanne K. Solem. It deals with everything from food preferences of all the common back yard visitors to coping with squirrels and other undesirables at the feeding station. Although its basic reference point is Maryland's piedmont, much of the information has universal application.

Too large for the telephone bookshelf and too heavy to manage with one hand while the other holds the phone, *The Audubon Society Encyclopedia of Birds of North America*, by John K. Terres, is in the next room with the oversize books—or, more often, lying open on the coffee table. It represents a major investment (or, as in my case, a loving gift), but it is a joy to read at random, and its photographs are superb. It is invaluable as a reference when grappling with such esoteric queries as "Do birds sneeze?" and "How fast does a peregrine falcon fly?" This is the source I have in mind when I tell a caller, "That's an intriguing question. Let me do some research and call you back."

Even as I wrote this, I was interrupted by a telephone call.

"Where can I go to see trumpeter swans?"

This one, as it happens, I can answer off the top of my head. But if the caller had only three of the books I have listed, he could have discovered for himself everything that I could tell him.

Any field guide would tell him that trumpeter swans do not frequent this area, but that their close kin the tundra (formerly whistling) swans winter along Chesapeake Bay and the east coast. When do they arrive? A quick glance at the bar graph in the Yellow Book confirms that they begin to trickle through in October, reaching peak numbers in mid-November. Where is the best place to find them? Claudia Wilds' book provides the answer: "Sheltered bays, rivers, ponds, cornfields. Eastern Neck, bays from St. Michaels to Cambridge, Md., West Ocean City Pond, Back Bay." And it gives precise directions to the prime spots.

But it was nice to talk to my caller and share in his anticipation. I left the phone with visions of swans in flight.

One Field Guide Is Not Enough

INVESTMENT COUNSELING IS NOT MY LINE, BUT I DON'T hesitate to share a bit of inside information with anyone who is interested. The best investment I ever made was the purchase of *Birds of North America*. The field guide (popularly known as Robbins, for its principal author) sold at $6.95 in 1970, and I figure the cost per hour of use has been about ³⁄₁₀₀₀ of a cent.

That is simply the cold economics of it, taking no account of the investment in physical and mental health and general sense of well-being that comes to those who choose to spend large portions of their time in the field following the birds.

The book I carry now, I have to admit, is not the same one I bought in 1970. It is a replacement—not of a worn-out guide, but of one that was lost in what was the greatest disaster of all my birding days.

It was in 1973, when my husband and I were still relatively inexperienced but thoroughly committed birders. The time had come to extend our range and study the birds of the west coast—birds that we had never sought out or even noticed in our pre-birding travels.

The trip came at a busy time, so we had little opportunity to do the proper homework in advance. This meant that we had to rely heavily on Robbins for on-the-spot identification. When we were driving, the book lay on the seat between us. When we left the car, it went with us, as essential as our binoculars, for we were strangers in a strange land, and any bird we encountered was a potential life bird.

On a Saturday afternoon early in the trip, we stopped at a market in a small town in the California Central Valley to pick up picnic supplies for the weekend. As we loaded them into the trunk, we were distracted by a noisy gang of magpies flying over the parking lot.

Were they yellow-billed or black-billed? If we had done our homework, we would have known that this was the territory of the yellow-billed magpie—but once again, we had to consult Robbins.

Satisfied with our identification, we moved on.

Two hours later, stopping at a roadside pond to examine an interesting congregation of shorebirds, we reached automatically for the indispensable field guide.

It wasn't there.

Shorebirds were forgotten as we emptied the car, trunk and all, in a frantic search for the missing book. At last we came to the awful conclusion: We had lost it at the magpie parking lot. One of us (and we carefully refrained from making accusations) must have left the book on the trunk when we got into the car. We had lost not only our guidebook but also our precious records—life lists and year lists, tucked inside the back flap.

What to do? We considered driving back. But that would mean four hours of driving time—and there was no assurance of retrieving the lost book.

Sadly, we studied the shorebirds, wrote down careful descriptions of the ones we didn't know, and drove on in a state of shock.

It was after six o'clock when we reached the next

Magpie

town. All the shops were closed, including the only bookstore. We were facing a guideless Sunday.

In desperation, we put in a call to the magpie market and waited while the helpful manager searched the parking lot and canvassed all employees before reporting, regretfully, that our book had not been found. He wished us a pleasant stay in California.

Pleasant? It was a nightmare. We were like travelers without a road map, a blind couple without a seeing-eye dog.

All day Sunday we looked at birds we couldn't identify with any degree of assurance—life birds, all of them, no doubt. Without that constant companion, we didn't know what distinguishing field marks to concentrate on. Without those handy distribution maps, we didn't even know what rarities might occur in the regions we were exploring.

It was past noon on Monday before we came to a bookstore, an oasis in the desert of frustration. We feasted our eyes on a table heaped with bird guides.

It was there that we bought the copy I carry today, and what a bragain it seemed! We would gladly have paid three times the price.

Then why didn't we buy three copies? Because we were stupid. Because we carried the "travel light" principle to a ridiculous extreme. We had invested hundreds of dollars in this trip, and we didn't have sense enough to protect our investment by carrying a spare field guide.

We are slow learners. It had taken us two years and three disintegrated field guides to learn that we couldn't afford the paperback edition—not for rugged use in the field. For occasional reference at home it may be a slight economy, but we feel more secure with good, sturdy hardcovers.

We have three copies of Robbins now, a very satisfying investment. One is kept in the car, one at the office, and one at home on the shelf with all the other field guides. (Since there is no perfect field guide, it is wise to have a variety for comparison purposes.)

In a sense, we had already learned the lesson: *One field guide is not enough.* After the California trip, the lesson had a new meaning for us. One copy of your favorite guide is not enough.

That was the greatest lesson of the whole trip. When you travel, always carry a spare. And never, never use the trunk or the hood of your car for a book rack. Not even for a minute.

Spish Power

SPRING CLEANING IN THIS HOUSEHOLD HAS TO WAIT UNTIL after the migration is over. March is too cold and too early. April and May are much too busy, with winter birds moving out, summer birds moving in, and wave after wave of migrants passing through. It would be unthinkable to spend precious daylight hours indoors and miss the last white-crowned sparrow or the first tree swallow; worse yet to miss the bobolinks on their brief stopover, or the fleeting visit of a blue-winged warbler, who may be here today, gone tomorrow.

June is soon enough for housecleaning. By then, the big show is over. The last blackpoll is on its way to nesting grounds to the north, summer residents are setting splendid examples of domestic responsibility, and the weary birder is compelled at last to turn to long-neglected household chores.

A good place to begin is the drawer that holds binoculars, bird checklists (used and unused), field-trip schedules, insect repellent, and scraps of paper with telephone numbers and mysterious coded directions ("Turn R at Power Plant .5 mi. L unmarked rd opp util pole Z143").

In the bottom of the drawer is a relic of those first days of bird watching: the Audubon bird call, which we, like most beginners, bought along with binoculars, field guide, and mosquito repellent in the conviction that this was one of the essential tools of the trade. We took turns practicing with it to make a variety of squeaky noises. Naturally, we assumed that all good birders carried bird calls and were proficient in using them to imitate all manner of bird songs. After a few field trips, we found that no one carried them, not even the trip leaders. Those who admitted to owning the indispensable gadget (at home in a drawer) usually said that they had received them as gifts but had never used them, even as beginners.

It's easy to understand why. In the first place, it takes two hands to operate the Audubon bird call, and those two hands are always busy focusing binoculars or leafing through the field guide. Moreover, the bird call is usually in the wrong pocket, or buried at the bottom of a pocket. Of course, it can be worn on a chain around the neck, but then it gets tangled up in the binocular straps. So the indispensable tool ends up in a drawer, where it is rediscovered annually and retained as a bit of nostalgia.

Experienced birders need no mechanical device to lure birds out of hiding. They have developed a simple "no hands" alternative known as "the spish"—a sound made with lips, tongue, and breath. Each individual has his own version of the "spish," and some execute it more successfully than others.

This was demonstrated to me one day at Dyke Marsh when marsh wrens, trilling persistently out in the cattails, were keeping themselves irritatingly invisible to watchers along the path. But two teenage boys, crouched down at the edge of the marsh, were able to coax the little singers right out into the open with soft whispering sounds. It looked so simple, but when I tried later to imitate their technique, I got no response at all.

According to field-trip etiquette, spishing is the prerogative of the leader. Followers remain respectfully silent and watch for results.

I remember when one of my first trip leaders took the group into a silent grove that suddenly came alive with chickadees and scolding titmice after a few quiet spishes. And I recall a virtuoso performance by Paul DuMont that brought a Swainson's warbler out of the depths of the Great Dismal Swamp of Virginia into close viewing range for some twenty eager watchers.

Not all birds are responsive to the spish. One would not expect to lure an eagle or an osprey in that manner, for example, and unfortunately the spish is totally wasted on shorebirds. It is most effective on songbirds with a high curiosity quotient. Chickadees, titmice, wrens, and nuthatches, as well as most warblers, will move in quite close to investigate a spish, and I have found gnatcatchers, catbirds, and towhees especially receptive, as are most species of sparrows, who will dart out of thickets and grassy cover for a quick look, then quickly disappear.

Only once has the spish brought trouble down on my head, in the form of an enraged magpie. My spish was not addressed to him; in fact, I had not seen him and didn't even know I was in magpie territory. It happened that I was between planes in Spokane, Washington, and I was taking advantage of the chance to see some life birds around the airport. With my binoculars in place, I was concentrating on some interesting sparrows scuttling around in the dry grass, trying to spish them out into the open, when I was dive-bombed by the magpie, who must have had a nest nearby.

The unexpected blow on the head was less traumatic than the raucous squall he uttered on impact. It was still ringing in my ears when I boarded my plane twenty minutes later.

Since then I have learned that it is not uncommon to have the wrong bird answer a spish. One lucky birder got a rare mourning warbler instead of an ordinary Carolina wren. Claudia Wilds once produced fantastic results with a spish intended for a white-eyed vireo; it was answered by a barred owl!

It is amazing how birds will respond to the human voice. But they also respond to mechanical devices. A friend who has a cabin up in the Blue Ridge Mountains relates the experience of one of his neighbors who was clearing trees on his property. His chain saw ran out of gas, and he stopped to refill it. When he turned the rusty cap on the gas tank, it produced a loud "Cronk!" that was promptly answered by a similar "Cronk!" from the nearby woods. He turned the cap again, repeating the sound. Again came the reply—and a wild turkey stuck its head up over a log to see what was going on.

What this man had discovered by accident was a highly specialized version of the Audubon bird call, effective only for turkeys. There ought to be a vast market for such simple devices as these to call out all kinds of rare and difficult birds. Hopeful birders would buy them, carry them once or twice, and leave them forever after in that relic drawer at home.

Beware of Fragile Authorities

A NON-BIRDING FRIEND OF OURS CAME BACK FROM A MEET-
ing of scientists in Colorado, where he had taken time
out to visit Rocky Mountain National Park. He couldn't
wait to report to us: "I saw a tamarisk!"

Our reaction was scarcely what he expected. "Lovely
tree. Didn't know they grew in the Rockies."

"Not a tree!" he exclaimed. "A *bird*. A rare bird!"

He granted he might have the name slightly wrong;
he knew it began with a silent *p*.

"Ptarmigan!" we shouted in unison, and he beamed
at our enthusiasm and obvious envy.

We were remembering all our efforts, several summers back, to find the elusive white-tailed ptarmigan.
How many times we had crossed Trail Ridge Drive, how
many times we had walked out over the tundra in futile
searches, before at last, on our final day of vacation, we
located a small flock feeding quietly on the ground, not
too far from the highway.

It was a triumphant moment, not only because ptarmigans were uncommonly scarce that season—the park naturalists said as much—but because their mottled coloring blends in so perfectly against the background of rocks and tundra vegetation that you can almost stumble over them without seeing them. Relatives of our familiar bobwhite, though somewhat larger, they spend more time walking than flying, and when they are feeding they walk along very slowly—so slowly that it takes an alert eye to detect their motion.

Then how could it be that this non-birder, without benefit of binoculars, had managed to find a ptarmigan on his first trip?

"Easy!" he said. "It was sitting on a post, right out in the open—a big gray bird—very handsome."

Envy turned to skepticism.

"How did you know it was a ptarmigan?"

The local scientist who was his host and guide had identified it. The scientist was not a birder but had lived in Colorado most of his life.

Doubt thickened the atmosphere. When in doubt, consult the book. Our friend looked at the white-tailed ptarmigan we showed him in the field guide and shook his head dejectedly.

"No, that's not it."

He riffled the pages quickly and found what he was looking for. "There it is!"

It was a Clark's nutcracker—one of the most common birds in Rocky Mountain National Park, a bird no tourist can miss. Noisy, screaming fellows, they live by their wits, haunting the scenic drive-outs where generous visitors offer handouts of peanuts and junk food.

Our friend was deeply chagrined, not because he had been mistaken but because he had broken one of the basic commandments of science: "Beware of placing trust in fragile authorities." His informant was a reliable authority in genetics, but a fragile authority when it came to bird identification.

Local residents who speak confidently about the wildlife around them are often grossly misinformed. I remember from my childhood in the midwest how common it was to hear farmers refer to all hawks indiscriminately as "chicken hawks." And my husband recalls the fragile authorities he encountered in Alaska who identified all bay ducks as "fish ducks."

A young mother I know, the ultimate authority in her young son's eyes, pointed out a flock of circling chimney swifts and told him to "look at all the bats." It will take time for the boy to learn that his mother's authority does not extend to the realm of birds and mammals.

No less an authority than an eminent scholar and professor of Old English once informed a group of respectful undergraduates, in an extracurricular setting, that robins, contrary to popular opinion, do not go south in winter.

"They go out into the fields and plaster themselves with mud and hibernate," he said with an air of authority that discouraged questioning.

As one of the respectful students, I suppressed a giggle at the image of thousands of muddy robins popping up out of the ground after the snows of winter had melted. But I could not suppress the question that no one else thought, or dared, to ask the good professor: Where did he get this information?

"Why, the mechanic at my garage told me," he replied, adding with complete solemnity, "and he's a damn good mechanic."

I said no more. After all, he was a damn good English teacher.

Lessons in Humility

THE TRIP LEADER POINTED TO THREE BLACK BIRDS BRACED against the wind in the top of a swaying sapling.

"I think we've got some rusty blackbirds here," he said, observing that they couldn't be red-wings because they had no epaulets, and they couldn't be grackles because their tails were too short.

"Besides," he said, "they don't sit upright like grackles. The first thing you notice about them is their horizontal posture. This is typical of rusties."

A gust of wind shook the tree, and the three birds flew up, stretching their tails to full length and revealing their true identity: common grackles, all three.

The trip leader grinned. "Now you've learned a lesson: On a windy day, birds don't always sit the way they're supposed to. And another lesson: Never take your leader's word for anything."

He was a good leader—one of the best—and he had learned long ago not to be unduly chagrined by mistakes in identification. His mistake was a reasonable one. It was the season for rusty blackbirds; it was appropriate habitat for rusty blackbirds; and he was *expecting* to see rusty blackbirds.

Anticipation is often the key to misidentification, as I learned to my embarrassment on a field trip I was leading in an area where a snowy owl had been reported. We flushed a barn owl, and in my excitement I called out, "A snowy!" I had forgotten how white a barn owl looks in flight—and wishful thinking made it appear even whiter.

On another occasion, I was quick to call the attention of a group to a phalarope, spinning in circles in shallow water, in typical phalarope style. The problem was, it wasn't a phalarope; it was a very ordinary dunlin, *behaving* like a phalarope. As one of my companions remarked dryly, "It takes more than one field mark to make a phalarope."

That, too, was a valuable lesson.

Birds don't always behave the way their species is supposed to behave. Gulls are not supposed to be flycatchers, but I have seen a ring-billed gull turn from his direct and purposeful flight to snap up an insect *en passant*. Harriers (marsh hawks) are not supposed to be fishers, but I once saw one hovering over the ice-laden Potomac in early spring, in much the same manner as an osprey. It had been a long winter, with fields and rodent runs covered deep in snow and ice, so the hungry harrier was forced to change his taste and his habits. There were dead fish floating among the ice floes on the river—enough to sustain him until the fields thawed.

In my back yard last winter, there was a junco that behaved like a nuthatch. Instead of feeding on the ground as any proper junco would do, he repeatedly flew against the trunk of an oak tree and climbed both up and down (admittedly for very short distances), clinging to the bark in nuthatch fashion. He had apparently discovered that this was a good place to pick up tidbits dropped by other birds from the suet feeder hanging on the oak.

But it is in the field, where distances and lighting and

Harrier

background can all contribute to deceptive appearances, that we learn and relearn the truth of one veteran's wry comment: "Birding is a humbling activity."

That it is.

I recall another leader, noted more for confidence than humility, who leaped from his car to train his binoculars on six silhouetted birds soaring high over the beach at Cape May.

"Frigate birds!" he shouted, his face flushed with excitement over what was surely an ornithological record for New Jersey.

The birds wheeled, and with the change of angle they were clearly identifiable as great blue herons, flying high on their migration route to the south—not displaced frigate birds from the Florida coast. The crowd of eager birders that had gathered saw the leader's flush of excitement turn to a deeper shade.

He was a seasoned and well-traveled birder. He had seen hundreds of frigate birds in their natural habitat, and hundreds of great blue herons, and he was understandably embarrassed at having mistaken one species for the other. But companions were quick to console him with tales of classic blunders, including the story that is frequently told in birding circles about Chandler Robbins, whose field guide is carried in thousands of field-jacket pockets and whose reputation is unassailable. But even Chan Robbins—so it is said—once mistook a great blue heron for a buffle-head. It was at some distance, you see, and against a confusing background. . . .

It happens to the best of birders, and there is no insurance against it. But there are precautions. My own rule for calling a rare bird (adopted after the incident of the barn owl) is: "Look twice and count to ten."

A wise novice will substitute questions for declarations: "Is that a Carolina wren?" or (in tentative tones), "Could I possibly be seeing an ivory-billed woodpecker?"

This approach may lack spontaneity and excitement, but it has the charm of humility, a quality highly respected among veteran birders who have learned it the hard way.

PART THREE

Views from the
Window

Birds of Melody Lane

MELODY LANE IS FOUR BLOCKS OF MARYLAND SUBURBIA with rolling terrain and wooded lots and a decent distance between houses. It is ten miles from the White House as the crow flies, or, more appropriately, as the gull flies, for we are on the direct commuting line of the ring-billed gulls that congregate on the Mall and the Ellipse, making daily trips to scavenge at the landfill several miles north of us.

More important, Melody Lane is only a mile from the Potomac River, a major migration route in spring and fall.

I do not know all my neighbors, but I think it's safe to assume that I am the only woman on Melody Lane who wears binoculars while doing her housework. I learned long ago that I missed too many bird views by having to run and get binoculars out of a drawer. So now I keep them close at hand, indoors and outdoors, whether I'm pushing a vacuum cleaner or a lawn mower. I want to be prepared for a glimpse of any bird, common or uncommon, that visits our half acre.

In fourteen years I have seen ninety-two species on or from our property—not counting the yellow-throated vireo found dead beneath the living room window, the only casualty we have discovered in all these years. This is surprising, considering the high ratio of glass surface on our frame house, which gives us inviting views of the woods and gardens but also presents hazards to birds. I think our slothfulness saves many bird lives; our windows are rarely washed more than once a year.

But through them we have seen woodpeckers and warblers, wrens and hawks, kinglets and thrushes. It is exciting to go out on field trips to hunt for seldom-seen birds, but there is nothing like seeing a red-headed woodpecker from the breakfast table, or a hermit thrush from the kitchen window. My favorite birds are the ones I see every day in every season.

During migration, spring and fall, anything can happen, and so the binoculars are always close by—on the table at mealtimes, on my desk as I work, or around my neck when I'm moving from room to room, doing routine chores. I always have a feeling that there is a great show going on outside my windows, whether I see it or not.

I prefer to see it.

One March day I was the unnoticed witness to the elaborate mating ritual of a pair of pileated woodpeckers only thirty yards from the house. I had often seen them singly, but it caught me by surprise to see the two of them clinging to the bark on a tulip poplar, only two feet off the ground and on opposite sides of the trunk. For some time they played peek-a-boo around the trunk, their incredible red crests flashing in the morning sun. Then the male (easily distinguished by his red "mustache" marks) emitted a loud cackle and ripped off a chunk of bark, tossing it grandly over his head.

The female was equal to the challenge, if challenge it was. Without a sound, she tore a piece of bark from her side of the tree and threw it to the ground. Anything he could do, she could do just as well.

After a few minutes of the bark-throwing display, the male hopped down to the ground and the female did likewise. Facing each other, about six feet apart, they bobbed their heads and swayed back and forth in another game of peek-a-boo, with a make-believe tree between them. When the male tired of this act, he flew to a nearby oak. Again, the female followed, after appropriate hesitation, and the bark-throwing ritual was repeated.

A Peeping Tom with binoculars, I watched until they flew deeper into the woods, to the tune of the male's triumphant cackle. I had happily frittered away a half-hour of a bright spring morning.

The distractions are greatest in winter. This is not the dull, dreary season when all the birds have "gone south." Where I live *is* the south to many species, as well as home to many birds that stay with us throughout the year: bluejays, cardinals, chickadees, titmice, Carolina wrens, and mourning doves. Winter or summer, we can depend on the mockingbird—as he depends on us, for daily rations of raisins.

My next-door neighbor, knowing of my interest in birds, asked me curiously about "that gray bird that hangs around our back yard." I had to think hard—first because it didn't occur to me immediately that anyone could live here for ten years without becoming acquainted with the mockingbird; and second, because I can't think of him as a *gray* bird. His colorful personality and virtuoso musical performances negate all concepts of grayness.

When I was growing up in Illinois, mockingbirds had not yet extended their range to that part of the country, so I knew them only through reading romantic fiction of the land, somewhere to the south, where the breezes were scented with magnolias and honeysuckle and the air was filled with the magnificent music of the mockingbird. I never dreamed that I would ever see this fabled bird—much less have one screaming at my window every morning for a "quick fix" of raisins to satisfy his addiction. So great is our familiarity with each other that when I put the raisins on the window sill, he swoops down impatiently, hardly waiting for the window to close.

Cardinals, too, are with us all year—usually traveling in pairs. When I see the subtly plumaged female, I know that the brilliant male is not far off. His color is most striking and cheering against the winter's snow. And he is the one who first announces the arrival of spring. Louis Halle noted years ago, in his timeless *Spring in Washington*, that the season actually begins on January 25th with the cardinal's spring song. I have heard it as early as January 11th on Melody Lane, and its message is more reassuring than that of the ground hog.

Juncos—the little charcoal sparrows with pink beaks—show up in October and brighten the backyard through the winter. I have a special fondness for these busy little ground feeders, recalling them from childhood. We called them "snow birds," appropriately enough, because they appeared with the first snowfall, which in Illinois was usually mid-October. And I remember in the depth of sub-zero weather having hot cocoa and oatmeal cookies in a cozy cave we had dug in the drifted snow, while juncos fed on the crumbs we scattered for them at the mouth of our cave.

In those days I had no binoculars. I didn't know the difference between a Carolina and a black-capped chickadee. I thought *all* chickadees were black-capped, and that all titmice were tufted. I had never seen a white-throated sparrow nor heard its high, lyrical "Poor Sam Peabody, Peabody, Peabody." Now they are wintertime regulars in our back yard, feeding on the ground with the juncos. I scatter seeds on the patio to lure them close to the house and keep my binoculars handy to bring them even closer into view.

Once, after a heavy snowfall, two field sparrows found their way to our back yard in their quest for food, and on the same day I spotted a white-crowned sparrow mingling with my little flock of white-throats on the patio. These are not everyday sights on Melody Lane, and I would hate to miss them.

Chickadees

People in Glass Houses

PEOPLE WHO LIVE IN GLASS HOUSES SHOULDN'T WATCH birds. Not if they expect to get anything else done.

It took me forty-five minutes to make the bed this morning. The trouble is, the bedroom has big windows, and I made the mistake of pausing to glance out at the back yard and the woods beyond, aglow with the warm brown of fallen leaves and still wet from a day of unseasonable rain. There was a temperature drop in the night; I could tell from the shrunken leaves of the rhododendrons and the thin fingers of ice in the bird bath. A pair of house finches was perched on its edge, drinking the chilled water.

The house finches are always with us now. Only a few years ago they were rarities. Common enough on the west coast, they were not even included in Peterson's earlier guide to the birds found east of the Rockies. But now they are successfully established in the east—and in our yard. They nest in the Chinese fir tree at the corner of the house and have practically displaced the house sparrows, which causes us no regret. I enjoy their bubbly song, but I seldom give them a second glance except to make sure that I'm not overlooking a purple finch among them.

It was not the finches that captured my attention and kept me frozen at the window with a pillow still clutched in my hands. I was held hypnotized by a scene of perpetual motion, like a complex piece of kinetic sculpture in which all the moving figures were birds.

Such numbers of birds! The population had quadrupled overnight.

Automatically I began counting—a compulsion birders suffer—but the restless flitting about made an accurate count impossible. Juncos were everywhere, at least sixteen on the narrow strip of lawn, running around like little gray mice. The flower beds were alive with them, and back in the woods wherever I looked I saw them scratching in the leaves, pouncing energetically with both feet and kicking debris aside with an impatience that gave a sense of urgency to their quest for food.

Some of the pouncers were white-throated sparrows—far more than the half-dozen that were feeding tranquilly on the lawn only yesterday. These newcomers—young ones with their lovely beige-and-brown striped heads, adults with bolder brown-and-white striping and bright yellow lores gleaming like little headlights—all were ravenous, and in such a hurry, as if this would be their last chance to eat before . . . before what?

Did they know something our meteorologists didn't know? Snow was not in the forecast, but this was the flurry of activity that often presages a storm.

Hyperkinetic chickadees zoomed from feeder to feeder, even attacking the suet, two at a time. The downy woodpecker and his lady displaced them only temporarily, but when the formidable red-bellied woodpecker appeared to claim the suet all for himself, they withdrew to the hanging feeder to console themselves with sunflower seeds, which they had to share with house finches, titmice, and three more chickadees.

The titmice, eight of them in all, darted nervously from feeder to feeder, making quick stops at the peanut butter station, then snatching sunflower seeds to dissect on a nearby branch. The goldfinches, more placid and leisurely, took up residence on the plastic cylinder and patiently sorted out seeds, rejecting three out of four and dropping them casually to the ground to be picked up by opportunistic squirrels and cardinals.

The cardinals, too, three pairs of them today, seemed relatively placid, not as frenetic as the juncos and sparrows. Did this mean they had traveled a shorter distance? Or that they were planning to stay with us longer? I did not know. But I noted their bright, fresh colors and recalled how scruffy and miserable our resident cardinals had looked during the molt season last September. Was that hard on their morale, I wondered, to go about looking so tacky?

These and other imponderables wandered through my mind as I followed the ever-changing scene.

Why were there no bluejays?

Why were the finches ignoring the thistle feeder to concentrate on sunflower seeds? And if they preferred sunflower seeds, why did they throw so many out? How did they determine which seeds were acceptable, which unacceptable? And why were their rejects fit for cardinal consumption?

One can find time to contemplate many important issues while a bed is waiting to be made.

Why were the chickadees so eager for suet? They seldom bothered with it; but today they watched for opportunities to snatch a quick bite when the woodpeckers abdicated. The female red-belly, I noted, was just as aggressive as her mate in defending the station. (Were they really mates? I wondered. They never appeared at the feeder at the same time. While one fed, the other waited and watched from a respectful distance back in the woods. Is this a matter of protocol?)

A white-throated sparrow, one of the immatures, ran the length of the rail fence and came to an abrupt halt at the rosebush to pick off an insect. Had he targeted it at a distance of sixteen feet? Or had he just spotted it in passing?

A chickadee investigated a crevice in the corner fence-post. Why did he look all wet and ruffled? No bird, except for the two house finches, had approached the bird bath while I was watching. I found the answer on the patio down below the window, where a shallow clay pot had been carelessly left on the wrought-iron table to collect water and dead leaves. A junco was splashing energetically in it, while a goldfinch perched on the table rim, patiently awaiting his turn.

Why did they feel the need of a bath on this chilly morning? And why did they prefer the clay dish to the metal bird bath? Probably because the metal was too cold for comfort, and they didn't care for slivers of ice in their bath.

As I pondered on this, and the need to install a water heater in the bird bath, the whole kinetic sculpture came to a halt. Nothing moved in the whole back yard. Nothing moved in the woods, except a pair of squirrels chasing each other around a tree trunk.

There wasn't a bird in sight!

Searching, I spotted just one: one of the red-bellied woodpeckers, profiled on a diagonal branch deep in the woods, perfectly motionless. All the others had vanished, and I hadn't even seen them fly.

Where had they gone? And why? Was there a hawk in the neighborhood? Looking up, I saw a lone crow flapping leisurely above the bare treetops. Surely they couldn't have mistaken it for a predator.

The crow disappeared from view, but the yard remained deserted. For several minutes I watched for signs of life, then turned back to the unmade bed with all those unanswered questions stirring in my brain.

Overriding them all was this one: What if I hadn't looked out at all, until just this minute? I would have thought it was a dead, dull winter day.

When I looked at the clock I was sure I was misreading it. If I had a windowless house, I could get my work done in half the time, or less. I would speed through it, so that I could get outdoors and watch the birds.

Woodpeckers of All Sorts

OUR NEXT-DOOR NEIGHBORS HAD HARSH THINGS TO SAY about a downy woodpecker that persisted in drilling holes in the side of their house. They finally solved the problem by nailing a piece of shiny metal over the newest drilling. This seemed to discourage the downy.

Their experience is not uncommon. In fact, this is the second time we have lived next door to a house that was besieged by downies. Why our own frame house is immune, I can't imagine—unless our generous offerings of suet during the winter buy us protection.

It also buys us entertainment, so we keep an ample supply in the freezer and portion it out among three separate wire-mesh suet holders. These attract starlings, unfortunately, but they also attract a more desirable clientele, including various woodpeckers.

The downies, smallest and commonest of our local species, avoid us in the summer, but in winter a pair of them visits us daily to feast on our handouts. They have become so tame that they will perch an arm's length away, scolding impatiently, while I replenish the feeder;

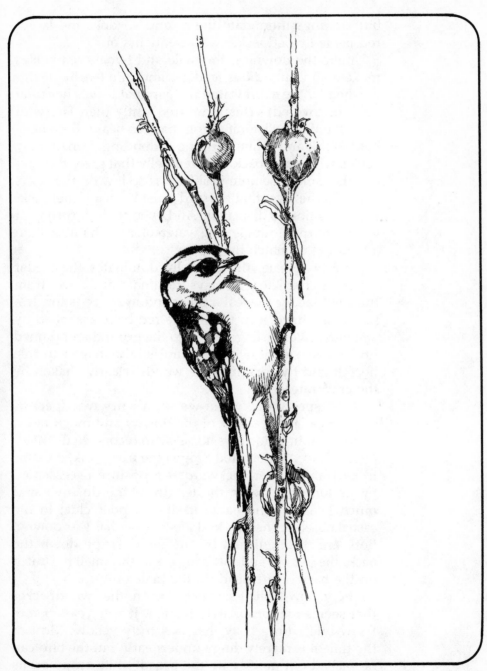

Downy Woodpecker

but starlings intimidate them, and so does the larger red-bellied woodpecker who frequents our woods.

Unlike the downies, the male and female red-bellies make solo visits to our feeders, and She (easily distinguished by the abbreviated red cap that leaves her forehead uncovered) visits more frequently than He (with his full red cap glistening from nape to beak). Both have bold black-and-white striping extending horizontally across wings and back. The red belly that gives the species its name is seldom visible. It is so low on the belly, between the legs, that the bird must be in a rather awkward position to display it. And even then, it turns out to be a disappointingly pale watercolor wash rather than a bold red to match the crown.

Male or female, the red-belly dominates the feeder scene, often evicting bluejays, cardinals, and doves from the seed feeder to steal a few sunflower seeds for dessert. But I have seen the female red-belly assaulted by an aggressive starling, forced to the ground and pinned under his relentless claws, until she managed to free herself and fly back into the woods, clearly shaken by the encounter.

It is a special day when we see a hairy woodpecker, which is a large version of the downy and much rarer. Even without binoculars it is easy to recognize the hairy by its stance. Silhouetted against the tree trunk, it seems to be leaning over backwards—a posture necessitated by its long bill, twice the length of the downy's and much heavier. The name itself is a poor clue; to the casual observer, neither bird looks either hairy or downy. Both are distinguished by the white stripe down the back, the pepper-and-salt wings, and the small red patch on the back of the head (in the male only).

The yellow-bellied sapsucker is another woodpecker that seems inappropriately named. It was years before I saw one with a belly that was truly yellow. Most of the time it is merely dingy underneath, but the bird can be picked out quickly by the broad white stripe on its black wing, as well as by its red forehead (to which the male has added a red necktie). These are the birds that perforate the trunks of fruit trees with rows of neatly spaced holes, which are rarely harmful to the tree. In fact, the sapsuckers help to free orchards from harmful larvae and borers. We see them only in winter or in spring and fall migration, en route to and from their nesting places farther north or in the higher elevations of the Appalachians to our west.

The common flicker is indeed common, especially in spring and fall, and he shouts his name, "Flicker, Flicker, Flicker!" Much less common in winter, he sometimes appears on the ground under the suet feeder where he picks up scraps dropped by the messier eaters. His call—a loud, raucous cackle—is similar to that of the pileated woodpecker, which, oddly enough, is a much more common sight in our woods, although it is generally considered a shy bird. I know of two pairs living on Melody Lane, and I hear them more often than I see them. Their drumming noise is unequaled by our lesser woodpeckers, unmistakably the work of a very heavy beak. They range widely in search of decayed trees that harbor tasty beetles and frequently visit our woods on their rounds. Apparently they find an abundant food supply, for I have never seen them at our suet feeder, although I have had reports from suburban friends who have enjoyed the luxury of their company at feeding stations on a regular basis.

And a real luxury it is to have this magnificent bird, the largest of our resident woodpeckers, right in our neighborhood. It is the next best thing to the extinct ivory-billed woodpecker, which we will never see. Fortunately for us, the pileated (whose fancy name simply means "crested" and is preferably pronounced "pie-lee-ay-ted") is not on the endangered list. Its life would be easier, however, if owners of suburban property would not be so quick to remove dead trees from their woods.

The woodpecker that I knew best as a child is the one

that I see least often in Maryland. In the midwest, red-headed woodpeckers were as common as robins. There was one on practically every telephone pole we passed on the way to school. In the east, where they used to be more abundant, their decline has been blamed on the growing population of starlings that competes aggressively with other cavity-nesters.

There are scattered colonies of red-headed woodpeckers in the state, but they tend to move about unpredictably, abandoning one favorite site after a few years and showing up elsewhere after an apparent absence. Melody Lane has never been on their preferred list. So it was a matter of great excitement when I saw this old friend from my kitchen window, perched high in a tree across the way.

What a handsome bird! All the male woodpeckers in this part of the country have *some* red on their heads—but here is one whose whole head has been dipped into the paint bucket. What could we possibly call him but red-headed woodpecker?

He rested long enough to give me time to appreciate him with full benefit of binoculars. Even as I admired his elegant tailoring of black and white, I was hoping that he might be joined by a mate. But no traveling companion appeared, and suddenly, with a flash of his broad white wingstripes, he was off—the first and only red-headed woodpecker I have seen on Melody Lane.

The Watchers and the Watched

I FEEL THAT I AM UNDER CONSTANT SURVEILLANCE. My home is not my castle—or if it *is* my castle, it is beleaguered, for they are watching it. Great numbers of them.

When I look out from my fortress I do not see them. But I know that they see me.

Their bolder scouts know just where to find me at any hour of the day. When I turn on the kitchen lights at 7:00 A.M., two mockingbirds come sailing straight to my window to harass me and collect tribute. If I am behind schedule, they seek me out, screaming rudely at the bedroom window on the opposite side of the house.

The others do not reveal themselves so readily. Looking out over the icy, barren landscape of the back yard, I think of my husband's word: *unproductive*. That's what he says when we are walking along the towpath and find it eerily lacking in signs of birdlife. "This is unproductive," he proclaims, and proposes to walk elsewhere because he is convinced that there are no birds to be seen here.

This is where we differ. Even though we don't see them, I know that they are there, people-watching from their hiding places. I know because I have seen it happen on our own grounds.

I go out to pour hot water into the frozen bird bath. A lady cardinal appears, waiting for a drink, and although I do not see him, I know that her mate is not far off.

Next I replenish the suet feeder, and before I have finished, the downy woodpecker is looking over my shoulder, urging me to hurry. He wants to get his share before the big red-bellied woodpecker comes to dispossess him.

Subliminally, I hear a goldfinch query as I pour out sunflower seeds. A bluejay gives the chow call, and there are sudden fluttering sounds all around me. I throw a generous portion of mixed seed on the frozen turf for the ground feeders and retreat to my castle.

Before the door is closed behind me, they have closed in. Goldfinches, titmice, and chickadees are clustered on the hanging feeders; jays, doves, and cardinals are vying for places on the platform. A Carolina wren runs along the rail fence and nearly collides with a cardinal. The red-belly has taken over the suet station, while a pair of nuthatches lurks beneath it, ready to catch the morsels he drops. Two crows move in, bouncing as if on springs as they alight, without disturbing the throngs of juncos and white-throated and song sparrows. Squirrels come out of the woods to mingle with the crowd.

They have all appeared out of nowhere. It is a feat of magic.

Now I can settle down to work, satisfied that I have bought peace for my day. The watchers are too busy to notice me.

But someone is watching the watchers. He zooms out of the woods so fast that at first I am conscious only of a brown shadow. It swoops low over the ground, confusing and scattering the infantry. My eyes follow the shadow as it makes a quick pass through the back yard and over the bamboo hedge and disappears in my neighbor's trees.

The brown shadow is a sharp-shinned hawk, out looking for breakfast. He did not get it in my back yard—not this time. But he was probably lurking off there in the trees, planning another attack.

In a quick shift of gaze, I discovered that the arena was suddenly deserted. Not a bird was in sight.

I picked up binoculars and searched the area for the hawk and his prey. Unproductive. There was not a move, not a sound.

Minutes passed. Then suddenly the silence was split by a single triumphant note, the "all clear" signal of an unseen bluejay.

The voice became a shape, and all the other familiar shapes reappeared without ever revealing their hiding places. With serenity restored to the scene, the watchers and the watched could get down to the business of the day.

Time for a Bird Break

ON THE HIGHWAY I OFTEN NOTICE CARS WITH BUMPER
stickers reading "Warning: I Brake for Animals."

In the same humanitarian spirit, I think I should warn
people who talk with me on the telephone during daytime hours: "I break for birds."

Friends have learned from experience to tolerate dis-
jointed conversations, but strangers and casual ac-
quaintances may sometimes wonder about that vague
lady whose responses are slow or even irrelevant. Some
may have been disconcerted by a sudden breathless
ending: "I'll call you back—'bye." Especially if *they* in-
itiated the call, and I don't know their number.

Unfortunately, I've never been able to invent a simple,
polite warning that would not require a more detailed
explanation than I am prepared to give as a preamble
to the average telephone conversation. It would have to
begin with the fact that I am a birder, then a definition
of terms, followed by a list of temptations that typically
come my way.

They would need to know that my telephone faces a row of windows that gives me a broad panoramic view of trees and sky, with a background of tall oaks and tulip poplars where chickadees, titmice, cardinals, blue-jays, and a variety of woodpeckers can be observed any month of the year. The foreground is dominated by the usual ornamental evergreens and maples, with the added interest of a crabtree that is cherished by the resident mockingbirds, as well as a birch clump, favored by finches. Just outside the windows is a stand of bamboo where small birds often find shelter in inclement weather.

The view includes a utility pole, from which our mockingbird stands guard over his territory, sings rapturous arias, and gives joyful leaps into the air as if in ecstasy over his own performance. The wires that reach out from the pole provide a convenient resting place for numerous birds, particularly the barn swallows that nest each summer on our neighbor's carport. One set of wires connects to our house and gives the mockingbird a place to sit near the window and scream at me for rations of raisins when he tires of his usual fare—or when he sees me wasting time on the telephone.

As if these are not enough distractions, the long cord on the telephone allows me to walk into the living room for a view of the backyard feeding stations and the woods beyond. There in a comfortable chair, with binoculars at hand, I can easily lose the trend of a conversation. I can even lose track of the time spent "on hold," listening to the background music from some remote ticket office, as I watch Carolina wrens flitting through the woods and woodpeckers taking turns at the suet.

From October to May the backyard scene is most interesting, but the real surprises usually come during migration seasons. Then it pays to walk from room to room with telephone in one hand and binoculars in the other, keeping an all-points watch.

A small bird drops out of sight into the bamboo thicket, and I ring off hastily to dash outside and track it down.

I find a small yellowthroat huddled near the base of the bamboo where it has found a safe place to rest.

A mourning dove on the wire across the street looks strange, and my attention wanders from a tedious recital of room measurements and decorating costs. The dove's head seems too large, the tail too broad. But the light is poor and the windows are not too clean. (I really must get those windows washed.) Laying down my pencil and picking up binoculars, I find that the "dove" is a yellow-billed cuckoo, the first I've ever seen on Melody Lane.

In spite of the momentous discovery, I keep a cool grip on the telephone. "Would you repeat that estimate, please?"

Another time, a flash of yellow disappears into a pin-oak just as I pick up the phone. "I'm just on my way out," I apologize truthfully. And I'm off—on the trail of a Cape May warbler right in my own yard.

With friends who share my interest in birds, I can be more frank. They all have had chats interrupted with gasps and exclamations over a tree sparrow in the back yard, a red-tailed hawk circling above the trees, a flock of cedar waxwings landing in the crabtree, or a pileated woodpecker flying right over the house. (This has happened more than once, but not with the same person on the other end of the line.)

I have never grown blasé about the pileated woodpecker, have never failed to look for his familiar outline when I hear his jackhammer attack on a tree trunk. He is without a doubt the most spectacular resident on our block, although not our most spectacular visitor.

That distinction belongs to another species that appeared when I was talking on the phone with a birding companion. I interrupted her in mid-sentence with an incredulous gasp.

"It's a pair of wood ducks! Flying right at the window!"

They were flying so low that I could see the female's white eye-ring and the handsome drake with all his colorful markings, even the gleaming red eye.

I thought they would surely hit the glass, but they zoomed up over the roof, missing the window by less than two feet.

Vaguely, I heard in my ear the same question that was buzzing in my head: "What are wood ducks doing over your house?"

It didn't make sense. The nearest body of water is an unattractive creek a half-mile away; the Potomac River, where wood ducks breed, is two miles distant. And to think they might be landing in our own woods!

"I'll call you back," I said.

But before I could hang up, they reappeared, circling back right over our rooftop. They dropped down in an oak across the street, where they presented an admirable target for my binoculars. The drake, settled on a horizontal branch, began to preen luxuriously, lifting his elegant crest with his beak and spreading it out to full advantage for the benefit of the admiring female, sitting on a branch a few feet below him.

Wood Ducks

And so they sat, until long after I finished my conversation, which was naturally prolonged by the diversion and my detailed eyewitness account to an envious friend.

Forty minutes later it occurred to me that my neighbor, who has at least a mild interest in birds, might like to know that there was a pair of wood ducks in her oak tree. I dialed the number with my eyes on the ducks.

"Would you like to see a wood duck? . . . Oh, sorry! There they go!"

She never got to see them. I would not have seen them myself if I had not been on the phone at just the right moment.

There was a time when I resented the intrusion of the telephone. But no more. I have learned to welcome that ring as an invitation to take time out for a bird break. Who knows what wanderers may pass my way?

Uncommon Grackles and Other Offbeat Birds

AMONG THE COMMON GRACKLES THAT VISITED OUR FEEDER last spring was a most uncommon grackle whose tail was striped in bold black and white, with shining black feathers down the middle and a contrasting white border on each side. It produced such a striking pattern that I couldn't help thinking that this accident of pigment was an improvement over the standard grackle design.

Such aberrations in coloring are not too unusual in the bird world. I have seen a hairy woodpecker whose red patch was misplaced from the back of his head to the crown; and a starling who came to our feeder to steal the suet we provide for birds of a higher class sported a single white tail feather. But he still looked and acted like a starling and presented no identification problem.

An offbeat junco I once observed might have sent a baffled beginner on a futile search through the field guides for a bird with this distinctive set of markings:

His slate color was accented by white wingbars; his black bib was mottled with white; and he wore a white collar that extended around to the back of his neck. In spite of all these abnormalities, however, he was unmistakably a junco, with pink beak and legs and slate background coloring, marred as it was. He was with a flock of juncos, and in size, manner of flight, and feeding behavior he was no different from the rest of the flock. The traits that made him remarkable in my eyes were apparently unnoticed by his fellows.

Anyone who spends much time observing birds is bound to encounter some odd specimens like these, and occasionally the greater extremes of albinism. The report of an albino robin in a suburban back yard will draw very few birders. This is a matter of puzzlement to non-birders, who can't understand why anyone who is willing to travel many miles to see a perfectly normal snowy owl, and even hundreds of miles to see a Ross's gull, is not interested in traveling around the Beltway to see an albino robin or sparrow.

In the study of birds, it is the species, not the individual, that counts; the normal is of greater interest than the abnormal. Birders are less concerned with obvious genetic aberrations than with the more subtle deviations within a species that sometimes make identification difficult. Very few birds fit the classic field-guide pictures perfectly, and some field marks—such as the central breast spot on the song sparrow—may be indistinct or totally absent. These fine points of identification can be a matter of animated discussion among birders, who are irritatingly indifferent to such rarities as albino robins.

The real interest may lie in the reactions of other robins to the albino. Are they tolerant, indifferent, or downright hostile? Not all behave admirably toward an oddity in their midst.

One fall, during a Cape May migration, I watched an albino in a flock of tree swallows. It was a pale beige bird, like a ghost swallow in a flock of thousands. The difference that was apparent to those of us who were watching was equally apparent to his traveling companions. As they swooped down over the Lighthouse Pond to drink, one bird after another attacked the odd bird, beating him with their wings until he was forced down into the water.

The flock swept on, leaving the pale ghost to drown—and leaving us to wonder about this evidence of discrimination in the bird world.

Mid-pond, the doomed bird struggled and flapped in the water, miraculously lifted off from the surface, shook its dripping wings, and followed after the flock. But in all probability he was still a doomed bird. If he rejoined the flock, or joined another, the episode would surely be repeated, with the ultimate success of the aggressors.

My next observation of an albino in the field was quite different. It was midwinter at Remington Farms on Maryland's eastern shore, where Canada geese were feeding in a snowy cornfield. Set apart from the main flock was a family group of three, one of which was a pale beige bird with shadowy face markings that identified it in muted undertones.

It appeared to be a young goose, somewhat smaller than the two adults that hovered near. It was their alert, watchful attitude that made the scene memorable. They did not eat. One on each side of their charge, they devoted their full attention to him, moving with him as he browsed. He fed placidly while they watched, tender and protective, as if they had something very special assigned to their care.

Cedar Waxwings
in the Snow

WINTER ARRIVED OFFICIALLY AT MELODY LANE ON October 17. We celebrate the beginning of the season on the day the juncos find their way to our back yard. We usually find them along roadsides and in farm fields at least two weeks before they seek us out, and as we pile up firewood for the winter we keep watching for their appearance at the edge of our woods.

They are quiet little birds, but I must have heard them above the rhythm of the rain. Something prompted me to look out, about mid-morning on that rain-soaked Sunday, and there they were, six of them, creeping about like little gray mice among the fallen leaves.

I reflected on the rewards of keen hearing, especially in this closed-in season of the year when the bird sounds are muted. But a birder's ears are always turned on, and even soft chips and lisps penetrate the walls and stimulate the inner ear. It is often a subliminal stimulus, producing an uncertain feeling that something has changed out there, something is moving, somebody spoke. The urge to investigate becomes irresistible.

That is when you look out and perhaps spot a brown creeper on the oak tree, or a flock of golden-crowned kinglets in the cedar, or evening grosbeaks on the feeder.

It was such a stimulus that forced me to look out, one February day, not at the back yard where all the action occurs around the various feeders, but out the front window where the view is mainly of bamboo and pine and an ornamental crabapple tree. This was where the action was. The crabapple tree was filled with cedar waxwings. The ground underneath it was covered with waxwings. If their high, sibilant notes had not registered on my subconscious, I would have missed this great visitation.

Waxwings are unpredictable in their wanderings. Some years they pass us by completely, but in most years we

Cedar Waxwings

see small flocks of a dozen or more, sometimes as many as thirty at a time. Never before had they descended on our property in such numbers. I counted 120 as they fed on the small crabapples that had fallen to the ground and the fruit that still clung to the tree.

Snow was in the forecast, and they ate ravenously as if they knew that this would be their last square meal before the world was buried in the deluge.

This was a sight that had to be shared. I called my friend Marilyn, a beginning birder who had never seen a cedar waxwing, and urged her to hurry over before the food supply ran out. She said it would take her fifteen minutes, and I returned to the window to watch the feeding waxwings.

The food supply didn't run out, but snow began to fall minutes later, signaling the end of the feast. The guests departed abruptly, en masse, lisping their thanks in a stuttering chorus of "see-see-see's" that I now heard quite clearly. They rested for a moment in the bare branches of a tall elm across the street, but by the time Marilyn arrived, they were all gone.

We had a consolation lunch and I described the show she had missed while we watched the snow accumulate rapidly on driveway and lawn and pile its furry coating on the trees. Within two hours the world was transformed, and we had forgotten the disappointment of the disappearance of the waxwings.

Then suddenly there was that insistent signal again —and we looked out to see the entire flock returning to the unfinished feast. There was a flurry of snow as they alighted on the draped branches and resumed their interrupted meal, oblivious to their audience at the nearby window.

In the gray light that had preceded the snowstorm their beauty had been striking enough; now, against the white backdrop, it was accentuated in every sharp detail.

Marilyn had been rewarded for waiting, and I was rewarded by her reaction.

"Their pictures don't begin to do them justice," she declared, glancing at the field guide on the table.

Indeed they don't. Even the best paintings and the most artistic photographs are poor substitutes for the real bird, and this is particularly true of the sleek, tailored waxwings. It is easy enough to portray the silhouette and the distinctive markings: the upswept crest, the bold black mask through the eye, the chrome-yellow edge on the tail, and the bright-red waxy formations on the wing-tips that are unique to the species and give it its name. But it is not so easy to capture the subtleties of the bird—the fine, silky texture of its feathers, the delicate blending of the softest tones of browns, beiges, grays, and blues. The cedar waxwing is a study in contrasts: both vivid and muted in color, both modest and bold in behavior. He eats voraciously, boisterously, sometimes reeling drunkenly from a surfeit of overripe fruit. But he never raises his voice above a whisper.

That whisper is enough to reach the ear of the turned-on birder.

The Mythical Siskin

It is surprising how many species of birds can be seen in a fairly ordinary suburban back yard. We started a list when we moved to Melody Lane, and although some of our best birds, like the scarlet tanager in migration and a stray bobwhite, have been seen only once, the list grew steadily. At the end of the first six years, it had reached seventy-five.

Number 75 was memorable, ending years of frustration and feelings of inferiority. It was a pine siskin.

It appeared on the thistle feeder the day before Christmas and came every day thereafter to share it with the amiable goldfinches.

Neighbors all around us had been feeding siskins for years, or so they claimed; but this was the first one to our knowledge that had ventured onto our property. And I think I know why. I think the word got around that my husband didn't believe in siskins. For years he maintained that it was a mythical bird invented by some practical joker to keep innocent beginners searching. Its proper name, he said, was a dead giveaway; who could believe "*Spinus pinus*"?* He subscribed to a conspiracy theory: The authors of all the field guides had agreed among themselves to perpetuate the myth.

When friends spoke of having flocks of siskins in their yards, he accepted the information as if they had reported a herd of unicorns.

It became embarrassing, after several years of active birding, to admit that we had never seen a single pine siskin. The usual reaction was a smiling, "Oh, you've seen them, all right—you just didn't recognize them."

If we didn't, it wasn't for lack of studying the pictures in the field guide, nor for lack of studying every suspicious finch and sparrow. We gave up.

Then one day a non-birding friend called and asked us (as if we were experts) to help her identify a flock of birds she was watching on her next-door neighbor's feeder. "They're streaky little birds," she said, "not as large as sparrows, and they have patches of yellow in their wings."

Her description sounded suspiciously like that of the mythical siskin.

"What kind of beak?" I asked.

"I'll see."

She looked out the window and reported that the beaks were sharp and thin, not at all like a finch or sparrow beak.

"And how about the tail?" I asked. "Is it square or notched?"

"Notched," she replied promptly. "Definitely notched."

That clinched it, and it was worth the five-mile trip to see the tame little birds feeding busily on the hanging thistle feeder, talking among themselves in wheezy syl-

---

*The American Ornithological Union has since seen fit to change this unlikely name to *Carduelis pinus*, which is much more appropriate. *Carduelis* is from the Latin *carduus*, meaning thistle—a favorite food of the siskin.

lables and paying no attention to the observers only a few feet away.

There were eight of them altogether, some on the feeder and others perched above it in the tree, waiting their turn. They were unobtrusive in their streaky, dusky garb, but in full sun they flashed the yellow wingbar like a badge. Some of them had corresponding patches of yellow at the base of the notched tail. But the overall color effect was so muted that I had to admit I might have overlooked them on a dull gray day.

So the pine siskin turned from myth to life bird, and as often happens when a long-sought bird is added to the life list, it suddenly appeared everywhere.

It was only a few days later that we spotted a large flock of them in a clump of birches as we drove through Gude's Nursery. Actually, we heard them first. The air was filled with their buzzy notes, and it was easy to locate the source of the sound. The flock was characteristically restless, flying up en masse as if at a signal, wheeling about, and then settling down again in the treetops to feed on the seeds of the birch trees.

That was a good year for siskins. The next winter we saw none at all. Like evening grosbeaks and crossbills —all, like siskins, members of the finch family—they have the reputation of being erratic in their comings and goings. They feed on seeds and buds of conifers and on the seeds of weeds and grasses. When their food supply is abundant in their normal range across Canada and the northern United States, they are unlikely to wander into my area. But in a winter of food shortages, or of prolonged ice and snow conditions that make food inaccessible, they head south, sometimes going as far as the Gulf States.

It was such a winter that brought Number 75, a lone straggler, to our thistle feeder. How he happened to find this particular feeder in his travels is one of those bird mysteries that constantly intrigue us.

A Kinglet Plays for a Captive Audience

THE WORST WEATHER CAN OFFER THE BEST BIRDING. So IN midwinter dedicated birders bundle up in padded layers and ski masks to go afield, knowing that there are exciting things to be found that will not linger until the balmy days of spring.

Over on Chesapeake Bay there are snow buntings at Sandy Point and tundra (whistling) swans at Eastern Neck. On Maryland's eastern shore, there are canvasbacks on the Choptank River, thousands of Canada geese, as well as snow geese and wintering ducks, at Blackwater National Wildlife Refuge, and purple sandpipers on the Ocean City jetty.

And of course there is always the chance of sighting an eider, a red-necked grebe, or a stray harlequin duck from a deserted, wind-swept beach.

Winter cold is no deterrent. But a winter cold is something else. When the head swims, the vision blurs, the nose drips, and the throat rasps, even the most foolish birder knows it's time to leave the chase to others.

It was such a cold that kept me indoors on a February weekend enjoying the pleasures of a crackling fire, a warm blanket, and a view of the busy back yard where familiar birds gathered. "Comfortably sick," as our old family doctor would have said, I could be content as long as there was someone to brew fresh tea, stoke the fire, and keep the bird feeders well supplied.

Through teary eyes I watched the customers flock in: dark-eyed juncos and white-throated sparrows on the ground; cardinals, mourning doves, and bluejays taking turns on the platform; chickadees and titmice on the hanging feeder; goldfinches on the thistle feeder; and a succession of starlings and woodpeckers on the suet feeder on the oak tree.

A Carolina wren appeared at the base of the oak to pick up suet crumbs dropped by careless eaters. Above it, a much smaller bird fluttered around the suet cage. Its size and behavior were enough to identify it immediately as a kinglet.

Our smallest bird (next to the hummingbird, which is not here in winter), the kinglet is a tiny dynamo of nervous energy, flitting and fluttering and flipping around in rapid 180-degree turns. Like the hummingbird, except for a much slower wingbeat, he hovers in mid-air as he feeds.

This was the first time I had ever seen a kinglet feeding on suet, and as he persistently picked morsels from the wire mesh without ever alighting on it, I marveled at his appetite as well as his agility.

It was not until he rested, ever so briefly, that I could determine that this was a ruby-crowned kinglet—not by the presence of the ruby crown (which he seldom shows in winter), but by the absence of a golden crown that would have been distinct even at that distance. Two days earlier I had seen a dozen golden-crowned kinglets in the cedar, their bright topknots gleaming against the dark-green foliage.

This little fellow was all alone, and he entertained me with his acrobatics off and on throughout the day, sometimes disappearing when the downy or red-bellied woodpeckers took over the suet feeder, sometimes dropping down below them to glean scraps they dropped on the ground and nearby shrubs.

Binoculars were useless to my brimming eyes, so I had to be content with the blurred image of this little winter visitor in olive-green garb that looked almost golden in the gray lighting of that dull February day.

Occasionally my vision cleared enough that I could distinguish his wingbars, but I had to rely on memory to supply the characteristic eye-ring that gives the ruby-crowned kinglet that "look of innocent merriment."

Memory took me back several years to a stop on the Chesapeake Bay Bridge-Tunnel and a chubby little dicky-bird straight out of a storybook, feeding boldly on insects at the side of the road, just in front of our parked car. He was busy-busy-busy, too busy to be bothered when I opened the door. But he paused a moment and gave me a wide-eyed look, showing off his unique eye make-up: a half-circle of white above and a half-circle of white below, not quite meeting in the middle.

I didn't know who he was, but suddenly he flashed his jewel-like crest and introduced himself: my first ruby-crowned kinglet.

In the years that followed, I learned how rare it is to get a glimpse of that dazzling trademark, which is usually concealed by the male's olive crown-feathers. He displays it in moments of excitement and possibly to attract the attention of a female.

Once, on an early spring walk, I happened to be passing by a small willow sapling just as a flock of migrating kinglets dropped into it, only a few feet from my path. There were ten or twelve of them, hanging like ornaments on the still-bare branches of the willow, warming themselves in the sun. They were all males, I soon discovered, for suddenly—whether alarmed by my presence or merely practicing for the mating season—as if on cue, all of them simultaneously flashed their ruby crowns in a display that had all the impact of a twenty-one-gun salute.

My winter kinglet outlasted my winter cold. For two weeks in February he was at the suet feeder every day. Then, suddenly, just as I was getting accustomed to seeing him whenever I looked out, he was gone, and that small pleasure was missing from my day.

Kinglet

Winter Wind Brings a Messenger

BIRD WATCHERS ARE WEATHER WATCHERS, ADDICTED TO daily forecasts and hourly updates. We get special bulletins from southern Illinois, where our son lives, on approximately the same parallel with us, six hundred miles to the west. The weather he has on Saturday morning usually reaches us by Sunday morning, often to the discredit of local forecasters.

On a midwinter day that was unseasonably balmy here, he called to report that the thermometer outside his window read 14 degrees Fahrenheit. Then, having warned us of things to come, he announced rather proudly that there was a chipping sparrow in his back yard.

His pride was understandable. Not too long ago, he had declared that all sparrows looked alike to him, and he was leaving their identification to others. House sparrows and song sparrows he could manage, but that was as far as he planned to go.

The declaration was a familiar one. We had heard it

from others and had probably said it ourselves in our early birding days when we were doing well to separate the hawks from the vultures. Sparrows were just too baffling. But for anyone who keeps looking, there comes a day when even the sparrows begin to sort themselves out. And here was an enthusiast claiming a chipping sparrow as his own.

In midwinter, at 14 degrees, it was unlikely—and we told him so, as gently as possible. He was ready with field marks to defend his conclusion: rusty cap, brown back, clear gray breast with no streaking.

A sudden thought came to me. "Does it have a black spot on its breast?"

"Yes, it has!" (A note of surprise there, as if to say, "How did you guess?") "It just looks like a smudge of soot."

"Then you have a tree sparrow."

There was a pause for consulting the field guide, then the triumphant exclamation: "That's it!"

He was not in the least chagrined by his mistake or our correction. He had added a life-bird to his list—a life *sparrow*, at that.

That night we were awakened by a howling wind. By morning, the temperature had dropped to exactly 14 degrees. That in itself was almost incredible. But to stretch credibility further, the first bird we saw in the back yard was a tree sparrow, the first time we had ever seen one on our property.

There was a temptation to believe that the same wind that had brought us our son's weather had also brought us his new life bird; but rejecting the pleasant fantasy, we admitted that it was much more likely it had moved in from some closer point—like Gude's Nursery, for example, where we had recently seen a flock feeding on weed-seeds in the snow. Here the food was more abundant, and he could feed more comfortably, along with the juncos and white-throated sparrows, in the sheltered area near the house.

He was not a lone traveler. Two more of his kind appeared, and soon the ground crew consisted of twenty juncos, twelve white-throats, two song sparrows, and three tree sparrows. Extra rations were in order.

The cold wind had caught last week's snow in mid-thaw and crusted it over in a smooth glaze. Seeds thrown from the window rattled over the surface, and the sparrows went skiing after them, slipping and sliding out of control on the downhill slope.

From a warm, comfortable ringside seat—without the usual disadvantages of numb fingers, cold binoculars, and fogged lenses—we got a better view of tree sparrows than we had ever had before, and when the sun came out to spotlight them against the shining snow, we could discern subtleties of coloring that the field guides neglect. The central black spot on the clear breast is only one of many points that distinguish it from its warm-weather counterpart. Another characteristic, which we were able to note for the first time, is the two-tone beak: dark above, yellow below. We had already observed that the "winter chippy" (as some people like to call the tree sparrow) has dark legs rather than yellow, and that he has a bright rusty "whisker mark" as well as a rusty line back of the eye to match his colorful crown. He lacks the chippy's bold white eye-stripe—but he compensates by wearing striking white wing-bars and white borders on his tail.

Even without these finer points of distinction, it would be hard for one who is familiar with both species to confuse them at first glance. To the practiced eye, there are differences in size, stance, overall coloration, and behavior. The petite chipping sparrow creeps along on the ground like a little mouse, and when flushed from a path he flies a few yards ahead and begins feeding again. He is rather tame, and most observers agree that he is "a cute little bird."

The tree sparrow, noticeably larger, is not "cute." He is trim and elegant, with a more upright carriage. His back is a warmer brown, without the gray rump that marks the chipping sparrow. His pale breast, with its diagnostic "stickpin" ornament, has a buffy wash along the sides, and the same muted-gold tone can be seen beneath the tail when he tilts forward to feed—or when he is flushed and flies up into a tree for safety.

It is that habit that earned him his name. Tree sparrows nest not in trees, but on or near the ground, where they feed in flocks—often in field margins near hedgerows where they can make a quick escape to high perches in case of sudden alarms.

We had seen them often enough in winter, flying up ahead of us as we trudged across the frozen fields of Hughes Hollow, or, unaware of our presence, quietly picking seeds from weeds weighed down by snow. But whenever tree sparrows are mentioned now, we remember the blustery weekend when our son got a life bird—and we got a life picture of a graceful little bird skating on the ice in our back yard.

No matter that it was not the same bird, transported overnight from the midwest to Melody Lane by some feat of magic. There was magic enough in the link it gave us to that other generation, in another place, making the distance between us seem not so great at all.

Hummingbirds in the Snow

The north wind doth blow
And we shall have snow,
And what will poor robin do then,
Poor thing?

—Anonymous

THERE IS SOMETHING ABOUT A SNOWSTORM THAT KINDLES the protective spirit lurking in all of us, filling us with the overwhelming urge to gather everyone in under one roof and around a warm fire to share our comfort. From our shelter, we want to reach out to the shelterless. We want to believe that all God's creatures are safe and warm and well fed.

And so, as the snow fell silently outside and the fire crackled noisily inside, it was not surprising to me that others, just as cozily situated, should start worrying about poor robin out there in the snow. The telephone rang repeatedly, signaling widespread distress over the plight of poor robin, poor cardinal, poor chickadee.

What can we do for them?

Not all the callers that winter day were motivated by the protective spirit. Those who spend their days in offices are more likely to deal with academic problems than with the practical problems of survival that concern the homebound. There may have been something more than idle curiosity that prompted the question from a group whose members described themselves as "casual bird watchers," who wanted to know: "Do birds sneeze?"

Possibly they, too, were concerned about poor robin, possibly catching his death of cold. Or maybe they were recalling the old folk tune about the bluejay who "sneezed his head and his tail right off."

The question sounded frivolous, they confessed, but it was asked in all seriousness. After all, mammals other than man are known to sneeze; why not birds?

No one had ever raised the question to me before. I could say only that, as a somewhat more than casual bird watcher, I had never observed any bird activity that might be described as a sneeze. But with my curiosity aroused, I searched (without result) through all the books at my disposal and then made a few telephone calls to fellow birders and bird banders. All were equally intrigued by the query, but none had ever seen sneezing behavior that they had recognized as such.

I was still immersed in avian respiratory systems when the hummingbird lady called. Her voice registered deep anxiety.

"What kind of food should I be putting out for the hummingbirds?" she asked.

In a flash of memory, I recalled a man who had asked a similar question last winter. Someone had given him a hummingbird feeder for Christmas and he was eager to put it to good use.

"If I put out sugar-water," the voice went on, "it would just freeze."

True.

"Do you have hummingbirds?" I asked cautiously, enjoying the fantasy of swarms of ruby-throated hum-

mingbirds darting about among the snowflakes, hovering over a frozen birdbath.

The lady admitted she hadn't seen any for a while
and had actually seen only one in her life. It had hovered
over her flowerbed one day in mid-October, she thought
it was, and she had been *so* excited. But she hadn't seen
it since—a fact she attributed to poor observation or
mere coincidence, convinced that hummingbirds must
be all around.

The excitement of that single sighting had stayed with
her, and on this wintry day she had to wonder, what
would that poor little bird find to eat out there in the
snow?

"He's so tiny," she added helplessly.

It was a relief to her to learn that her hummingbird
was long gone to warmer climates. But her relief was
followed by a wave of incredulity.

"You mean they *migrate*—those tiny things?"

When I assured her that this is really true and shared
the astounding fact that they actually fly across the Gulf
of Mexico to their winter homes in Mexico and Central
America, she was momentarily speechless.

"Do they travel in flocks?" she demanded.

Migration to her meant large numbers of ducks and

Hummingbirds

geese traveling together in well-ordered squadrons. The idea of small birds striking out on their own into the wild blue yonder was almost more than she could accept.

"Unbelievable!" she kept saying. "Unbelievable!"

And of course it is. Even when you see it, and know it, you can't believe it.

Then a new thought came to her as she contemplated the sugar-water feeder she had bought.

"When will they come back?"

With the assurance that the hummingbirds would be returning as early as mid-April and that it would be reasonable to put her feeder out by the first of May, she was ready to start planning a garden full of hummingbird treats. She left the phone to study seed catalogs, not a bad activity for a winter day.

I turned back to the fire, envisioning the masses of phlox and petunias, lilies and four-o'clocks and trumpet vines that would brighten the lady's garden, where she would be keeping vigil for the return of her hummingbird.

Then out of the fire came another vision, totally delightful, a gift from the hummingbird lady whose eager questions had inspired it. What I saw was squadrons of hummingbirds flying in V-formations, their iridescent green wings flashing in the sunlight, their ruby throats gleaming like jewels, as they sailed over the sparkling waters of the Gulf of Mexico, thousands of them, all heading north.

The Bird That Isn't There

LIFE IS UNFAIR. IT SEEMS ESPECIALLY SO TO ANYONE WHO comes down with a worrisome bug at the tag end of a worrisome winter when everyone else is outdoors enjoying spring flowers and sweater weather.

From my bed, I listen to the sounds of advancing spring, but unhappily I can see very little of its progress. The high windows in the bedroom, designed for privacy rather than bird watching, offer only a limited view of the treetops and sky, and none at all of the back yard. If I'm forced to stay here much longer, I'll have to have mirrors installed at the window so that I can see what's going on outside.

Lacking that, I have to rely on my ears. At dawn, after a restless night, I start taking the roll:

Cardinals (always the first to sing out): emphatically present.

Song sparrow: here, singing an abbreviated song.

Mourning doves: present and mourning.

Carolina wren: cheerily here.

At breakfast time, chickadees and titmice join in; a starling squeaks; bluejays (probably two or three, sounding like a dozen) scream their presence; house finches set up an effervescent chorus, interrupted by the assertive voice of the mockingbird, who has probably just evicted them from his holly tree.

I doze and wake to hear the throaty gargle of the red-bellied woodpecker; the "yank, yank" of the white-breasted nuthatch; and a soft, musical twitter that at first tricks my foggy brain into believing that a pine warbler has finally come our way—until I remember that the juncos have fooled me before with their spring song.

All these auditory clues help me visualize the back-yard scene and ought to give me the sense that all's right with the world. But I have vague feelings of uneasiness, intensified by the sudden raucous racket of a gang of crows, much too close at hand.

Worries begin to take shape.

Are the crows stealing suet again, after all we've done to outwit them? Worse yet, are they thinking of nesting in our woods? They aren't the most desirable of neighbors.

Suddenly their noise stops. All noise stops. Even the mockingbird stops singing. The silence is oppressive. Is there a hawk lurking around? Or is the black cat, Midnight, trespassing?

In the silence, I can imagine all kinds of things gone wrong: The bird bath has gone dry; the squirrels have found a way to rob the squirrel-proof feeder and have eaten up all the sunflower seeds.

Apprehensions build up. Maybe it's the nature of the bug that has infested me, or maybe bird watchers are just natural worriers. Only yesterday an anxious woman phoned to ask what nesting material she should put out for the birds—as if they'd never find any without her help. And in the midst of our last snowstorm, another worrier called to ask if he shouldn't supply grit and pebbles for the birds at his feeder, to aid their digestion.

But, as I said, it was a worrisome winter. Not severe, but worrisome. And the silence in the back yard made me aware of what bothers bird watchers most. No matter what's out there, we worry about what isn't.

It was a winter of absences. Evening grosbeaks, absent. Cedar waxwings, absent (at least in our back yard). Pine siskins, absent. Red-breasted nuthatches, absent. All these are erratic and unpredictable, of course. But purple finches? Only an occasional two or three. Worst and most worrisome of all was the absence of white-throated sparrows. Normally, we expect to see ten or twenty of them, along with the always-abundant juncos, feeding on the ground. This winter they appeared rarely and stayed briefly, only one or two at a time.

What mysterious change had taken place?

Whatever it was, it was a local phenomenon—confined, apparently, to Melody Lane. There was no shortage of white-throats on the Christmas Count, no indication of an overall decline. And friends all around us, less than a mile away, reported more white-throats than juncos this winter. I don't understand it.

Too weak and weary to deal with imponderables, I try to focus on the morning paper. It offers no escape for the worrier. There on the front page is the arresting headline: OCEAN CURRENTS DEVASTATE BIRDS OF PACIFIC ISLE. Here is the story of a real disaster of a magnitude that is almost beyond comprehension.

> Almost all the 17 million adult birds on Christmas Island in the mid-Pacific have been killed or fled, leaving their nestlings to starve to death, according to a report presented to the National Science Foundation. . . .
>
> The "population crash" is probably the largest of its kind ever recorded, and the first near-total disappearance of a major bird population recorded on a tropical island. . . . Of the 19 species that were on the island, 18 are gone, including the world's largest sin-

gle population of sooty terns. . . Fourteen million of
them have disappeared.

The devastation on Christmas Island is described in
grim detail, where thousands of dead nestlings and a
few dead adults were found, giving evidence of mass
starvation and evacuation of terns, shearwaters, frigate-
birds, and other marine species.

What had happened?

Investigators of the ecological disaster were blaming
it on the *El Nino* weather phenomenon. The speculation
is that adult birds fled the island, not because of storms,
but because the reversal of ocean currents had swept
their fish supply into deeper waters, and they were forced
to move on, leaving their nestlings behind to starve.

It has, indeed, been a worrisome winter. My imagination is not powerful enough to picture the macabre
scene on Christmas Island, nor to encompass the loss
of *14 million* sooty terns. But I can at last stop fretting
about my little back yard and a handful of white-throated
sparrows.

Martin House for Sale

WE'VE GIVEN UP ON PURPLE MARTINS. FOR SIX YEARS WE'VE given them a fair chance, offering them attractive, rent-free quarters: 12 rm. w/balcony; exc. view, quiet res. area; conv., inside Beltway.

Year after year, we lowered the martin house (not always the same house; we tried various models and materials), cleaned out the offensive sparrow nests, and hoisted the house again, like a symbol of hope on top of its pole, waiting for tenants that never came.

The quarters were investigated once—and only once, so far as I know—by an advance scout who came in March on an inspection tour. That was five years ago, the year of the New Improved Asbestos Bungalow, which had proved its popularity and livability in other neighborhoods. In our neighborhood it was a first, and we offered it with pride and inflated hopes. This was going to be The Year of the Purple Martin.

And so it was—the year of the purple martin, the only one ever known to trespass here. He made his presence known, fluttering close to my window and hovering there, possibly attracted by the chatter of my typewriter. When I stopped to stare in amazement, he retreated, circled once around the asbestos house, and flew on—never to be seen again.

Like a teenager waiting for the telephone to ring, I watched that house day after day with growing feelings of inferiority. What had we done wrong?

My husband accepted it more calmly, but after all, he had never lived with purple martins. He didn't know what he was missing. In my childhood, there were always purple martins. No one went to great lengths to attract them; one simply accommodated them because they were there, and because they made such good neighbors.

They were friendly toward people and peaceable among themselves in their communal existence, and they were not fussy about architecture. We offered a variety of home-made wooden shelters, the ultimate being a replica of our own house, complete with dormer windows and asbestos shingles. My father, who had designed our home, built a scale model, and after construction was completed it occurred to him that he could remodel the model with enough partitions to take care of two dozen martin families. There was no doubt that it would be fully occupied.

The martins settled in quite happily, with minor competition from sparrows whose numbers were controlled by boys with BB guns, more often intimidating than lethal. Nevertheless, there were always a few brave sparrows that dared to nest in the mansion, and it was one of the first spring chores to clean out their debris in preparation for the martins' arrival. We knew they liked a tidy house.

In retrospect it seems strange that I knew the martins so well, and yet I knew so little about them. I didn't even know they were members of the swallow family, although their manner of flight should have told me that much if I had thought about it. I knew their habit of sitting in a row on telephone wires, chortling softly to one another, and occasionally darting out in turns to snap at an insect. I did not know that we owed them special thanks for keeping our lawn relatively free of mosquitoes.

I knew that the male scouts came early, handsome and respectable in their solid, iridescent purple, and that they would be joined later by the quieter gray-breasted females. These events and the appearance of the first fledglings were recorded carefully on the calendar—as well as the day in September when they all left en masse, after a great deal of conversation and commotion. I knew only that they were going "south"; I did not know that "south" was South America, or that they followed a route across Central America and Venezuela to their winter home in Brazil.

I missed them when they left. I miss them now, and I wonder why I can't have the pleasure of their company in my Maryland home, as I did in Illinois. What is wrong?

Is it the location? Some experts claim that martins don't nest inside the Beltway—but I doubt that a purple martin would be inhibited by man-made boundaries.

Is it the lack of a convenient water supply? Booze Creek is a half-mile away—about the same distance our Illinois martins used to travel to the nearest pond.

Are there too many obstructions to the flyway? Too many tall trees to impede their flight? Possibly. Surely we have placed the house in the most open space available, and at the correct height. There are convenient perching wires near at hand, and the mosquito supply is abundant.

Whatever the reasons, we've given up. Hope does not spring eternal—not at our age. Last fall we took the martin house down to repair squirrel damage. We aren't putting it up again this spring. We know it's a lost cause.

I'm sorry about that—not so much for myself, but for my husband, who grew up in the city without knowing what a purple martin was. At least I have the comfortable memory of lying on the cool grass on summer evenings when it was too hot to sleep, watching the sky for shooting stars and listening to the low background music of the martins murmuring their contentment.

Spring's Golden Rewards

EVEN BIRDS CAN PLAY THE GAME OF APRIL FOOL.

You hear the clear whistle of a bobwhite and trace the sound to a talented starling.

You hear the cry of a killdeer and find that it's only a mockingbird producing a very reasonable facsimile.

You hear a twittering like the rapid series of chips of a pine warbler or a newly arrived chipping sparrow— but it turns out to be a dark-eyed junco. These silent little gray birds of winter have suddenly found their voices, and they spend their days in music practice, not on the ground where you usually see them, but perched high in the trees as if poised and ready for the takeoff to the north.

Chickadees stop repeating their names endlessly and concentrate on their love song, the high, clear, "Fee-bee, fee-bay" that sounds quite unchickadee-like.

And those dingy little olive-drab birds that clung to the thistle feeder all through the winter months have disguised themselves in yellow as vivid as daffodils.

One of the greatest rewards of spring is that of watching the goldfinches get their color. Equal to finding the first bloodroot, the first spring beauty, or the first robin on the lawn is the excitement of seeing the first yellow goldfinch. It may be a newcomer, just arrived from the south to swell the numbers that have wintered here, or it may be a member of the flock that has been here all along, made suddenly conspicuous by his fresh new plumage.

Of course it is not as sudden as it seems. The prenuptial molt, as the ornithologists call it, is a gradual process. If you were watching closely, you noticed color changes in March—and even during the winter months you have observed that some of the goldfinches on the feeder wore touches of yellow. The adult males—those in their second year—are distinguished by their yellow shoulder patches, and their breasts are often washed with pale lemon. The first-year males lack this show of color, but they have the same black wings, barred with white, setting them apart from the duller females with their olive-brown wings.

During the molt, both sexes change their entire body plumage. Wings and tail remain the same. So does the little pink beak, which adds an interesting color accent. The female's body becomes a subdued yellow, but the male's new garb is anything but subdued. Contrasting with the luminous yellow is a rakish little black cap, tilted forward on his forehead.

Even before this transformation is completed, the male goldfinch begins exercising his vocal cords. During the winter, you heard little from him except the occasional surprised query, on a sharp upward inflection: "Meeee?" But on sunny days in March, he begins practicing his long, warbling song, softly and almost timidly at first.

The song, like his color, gradually becomes bolder, and by the end of April he is in full voice, singing his "long song" from the treetops and giving his distinctive flight call as he moves about. That song, translated in

Goldfinch

most books as "Per-chicoree," comes through to me as "Chic-chicory," a happy little song given as the bird bobs gaily along in his looping roller-coaster style.

There is something especially joyful about a bird that sings as it flies, and the goldfinch strikes me as one of our most joyful birds. Perhaps he appears so carefree because he has a long courting period before he settles down to domesticity, for the goldfinch nesting season does not begin until late summer, after most of the breeding species have launched at least one brood. There is nothing accidental about their timing. Goldfinches depend on thistledown for their nests and thistle seeds for their families, so they delay their nesting until the plants have matured.

Meanwhile, the sociable flocks of goldfinches go flitting about, conspicuous both by numbers and color. In early spring you see them adorning a leafless birch tree like bright Easter eggs hung from its branches. Or you may come upon them on a grassy lawn, rivaling the dandelions for color as they feed on the earliest dandelion seeds. Startled, they explode into the air in unison and go one their bouncy way with repeated calls of "Chic-chicory."

It seems to me a peculiarly appropriate refrain, for I have observed their special affinity for the chicory plant. We are accustomed to seeing them on thistles and sunflowers, and it is a memorable experience to see several little yellow birds clinging to a larger sunflower head, systematically stripping it of seeds.

But a goldfinch swinging on a stalk of blossoming chicory produces a color combination that is unexcelled in all of nature's schemes. Canary-yellow and chicory-blue: These are colors that sing to each other. It is worth going out of your way to see them, and in fact it would be a terrible loss to let the season pass without savoring this sight.

Once you have seen it, you can never again think of the goldfinch as a drab little bird, even in the dull depths of winter.

A Cat's Cradle for Birds

A COOL MORNING WITH THE INDEFINABLE SCENT OF AU-
tumn in the air inspires me to clean the bird feeders in
readiness for the coming season. It is pleasant working
under the maple tree, with brushes and pails of soapy
water and rinse water to make the chore efficient.

The birds seem to know what I am about. The devoted
cardinal couple watches from a nearby shrub; chickadees appear as if by magic out of the woods; and a pair
of house finches, now a familiar sight year round, perch
on the clothesline to supervise activities.

Overhead in the maple a family of tufted titmice gath-
ers to watch the process, buzzing excitedly over the
prospects of a free lunch. This is the second brood of
the season, and I sense that the parents have grown a
trifle weary of the endless responsibility.

Inside the house, the white cat watches with green-
eyed intensity. He lashes his tail vigorously when one
of the titmice drops down onto the clothesline, chattering impatiently. I have no doubt that the bird sees the
white cat, but he gives no sign of alarm. He understands

the pane of glass that separates them, so he can afford a show of bravado. He knows this is The Enemy, but The Enemy under glass poses no threat.

When they are both on the same side of the glass it is a different story.

Ordinarily, the white cat does not go outdoors, where he would be prey and predator, just as his ancestors were. I am unwilling to turn him loose to the mercy of the big dogs that wander, unleashed, through our neighborhood, just as I am unwilling to turn him loose to harass the birds that I lure to the back yard with offerings of food and water. So the cat spends his life on the inside looking out, cowering when a neighbor's dog passes by, arching his back and fluffing his tail at trespassing cats, and chattering his teeth at birds and squirrels.

In the summer, when his coat is shedding profusely, he goes into the world beyond the glass once a day when I take him out for a brushing. He enjoys this attention so much that he makes no effort to bolt and run, although he could break away very easily if he only realized it.

The birds and squirrels realize it, if he does not. They disappear and fall silent during those grooming sessions, but I know they are watching because they reappear on cue as soon as the cat is carried back indoors.

With the feeders all cleaned and rinsed, reassembled, and hanging on the clothesline to dry in the sun, I turn my attention to the captive cat. He is not shedding as much now, and the tufts of fur that float away on the breeze are smaller each day. I remember the early days of summer when fat wads of white, like cotton balls, decorated the back yard after the brushing routine.

One day in July, after the daily grooming, I was sitting on the screened porch with my coffee and newspaper when I became aware of a slight movement in the Chinese holly only a few feet away. A small gray bird was working its way surreptitiously among the lower branches.

Titmouse

I was surprised to discover that it was a titmouse, in a most uncharacteristic attitude.

In the first place, he appeared tuftless. With his crest flattened to his head, he looked smaller, less aggressive, more secretive, as if he were traveling incognito. His manner, too, was secretive. Silently, warily, he dropped to the base of the holly where white clusters of cat fur clung to the ground.

This was his objective.

Furtively, as if handling some irresistible contraband, he gathered it up in his beak, adding more and more to his collection until his face almost disappeared in a misty white cloud. It did not seem to obscure his vision, for he flew unerringly, with his head in the cloud, to his building site back in the woods.

I watched him make several trips that day and enjoyed a special delight in the private knowledge that the enterprising little bird was stealing choice nesting material from his unwitting enemy.

Now the titmouse family is silent as I finish the brief brushing. The plastic feeders are still too wet to fill with seeds, and it is still a little early in the season to start the feeding routine. But I feel a generous impulse toward the titmice, and when I take the cat indoors I raid the peanut butter jar in their honor, smearing gobs of it into the grooves of the log feeder. I hang it on its hook just outside the living room window, and by the time I am back indoors, two generations of titmice are buzzing their excitement over the bonanza.

They attack it with cool disregard for The Enemy, who flattens his ears to his head, scowls, and twitches his tail back and forth. The young titmice, getting their first taste of peanut butter, will learn quickly that this is a reliable source. They will learn, too, about the pane of glass that protects them from the white cat, who is their enemy—but neither he nor they will ever know that they were rocked in a cradle lined with his soft white fur.

Nighthawks Trigger Migration Fever

FEW THINGS ARE CERTAIN IN LIFE, BUT AT LEAST ONE THING I can depend on: If I look out the kitchen window at dusk on August 16, I will see the nighthawks coming over Melody Lane on their journey south.

(They might be there on August 15, but I never take the risk of looking. I am not eager to add any new variables to my life.)

Their slender pointed wings make a graceful silhouette against the darkening sky. Sometimes they fly low enough to show the white spots on their wings that are their trademark.

I go outdoors to watch them as they come over in groups of six or eight, never in the large flocks that can be seen over the Potomac, which is a favored flyway. But we are close enough to the river to get these small splinter groups that hear a different drummer—or, more likely, a different insect, for they feed in mid-air, emitting their peculiar nasal buzz-note between bites.

These birds have large stomachs requiring huge quantities of food, and their wide mouths are designed to scoop up any insect in their flight path, from small gnats to large moths.

You can tell when they pass through an insect cloud that is invisible from the ground. They change course abruptly for an in-flight gourmet meal, darting and circling in precision maneuvers, sometimes turning back to the north as if they had changed their minds about migrating after all.

Throughout late August and into September, the nighthawks put on their nightly show over Melody Lane and make surprise appearances over illuminated playgrounds and shopping malls, where insects clustering around electric lights are easy prey.

It adds a sudden zest to an evening shopping expedition to hear that familiar buzz and pause to watch the nighthawks enjoying a late dinner.

They do not always fly by night, having no compulsion to conform to the name we have given them. I have seen and heard them at high noon. If they are sensible, they rest during the midday August heat, and then they make themselves practically invisible, lying horizontally along branches so that they can easily be mistaken for the proverbial bump on a log.

But the very hungry, or the foolhardy, do go out in the midday sun to appease their voracious appetites.

Their evening flights over Melody Lane mark, for me, the turn of the season and the onset of that malady known to birders as migration fever.

I don't know why it takes the nighthawks to trigger an attack. There have been earlier signs. Swifts and swallows have preceded them in restless flocks, and great congregations of grackles have been passing over at sunset, clucking noisily on their way to overnight treetop roosts. Robins have reappeared in great numbers on suburban lawns. I have heard the katydid chorus at night swelled by the addition of crickets, and in the daytime I have heard the steady squeaking of titmice and the raucous complaints of the bluejays screaming, "Thief! Thief!" at the unseen marauder that has stolen their summer.

I know that over on the coast the great shorebird migration has been underway since July. For many birders, it is the shorebirds that spark the first symptoms of migration fever.

I call it Cape May Fever, and for me it begins when I look up at the nighthawks and realize that they could be traveling from as far north as the Arctic Ocean to the southern tip of South America. I think of all the other travelers and I become restless. My mind wanders easily.

But it always comes back to Cape May. Cape May— the southernmost point of New Jersey—*the* place to watch the fall migration. It is the jump-off point . . . land's end . . . last chance for food and rest.

They come in great numbers and varieties, especially when blown by a northwest wind. On a good migration day I have seen 500 broad-winged hawks and impressive numbers of kestrels and sharp-shinned hawks, with a few Cooper's hawks and an occasional peregrine falcon. I remember a bare tree adorned with eight species of warblers—plus a brown thrasher, two catbirds, a cardinal, and several red-winged blackbirds.

There was the day of the ospreys, when we counted forty—and watched a dozen of them all feeding at once on fish they had captured at Higbee Beach.

I remember ducks coming in for splashy landings on Lily Lake, while overhead flights of herons and egrets crossed paths with thrushes and cedar waxwings. I remember the procession of flickers passing over in silent single file; a woodcock dozing in the sun; and bluejays dropping to the ground, too exhausted to utter a cry.

It is not numbers on a checklist that make a Cape May migration unforgettable. It is the feeling of being a participant in this great mass movement. Nothing can evoke that feeling more effectively than the thousands of swallows that appear like clouds on the horizon. Suddenly the cloud overtakes you and you are in their midst, hearing the flap of their wings and their soft, breathless twitter as they swoop down past you. They circle over a pond, a thousand at a time, drinking and snapping at insects.

These are memories that fan the fever that starts with the sight and sound of the nighthawks. I felt it coming on unexpectedly one day when I was far from home, in Nauvoo, a sleepy little Illinois town on the Mississippi Flyway.

Nauvoo was baking in 100-degree heat and I was heading for a cool lunch when I had a sudden vision of the Cape May Lighthouse, like a mirage. What was it doing here in this midwest town?

The answer came in a harsh, buzzy note overhead. There they were, against the blinding noontime sky. Of course. It was August 16.

The Song of the Bluejay

CARDINALS ANNOUNCE THE ARRIVAL OF SPRING, BUT IT IS the bluejays who herald the first days of autumn. Nothing is more characteristic of the season than the gangs of jays that dash busily through the woods, uttering calls that vary from the "steel-cold scream" described by Thoreau to flute-like tootles of pure joy.

They seem to bounce on springs as they alight on feeders that have been empty during the summer months. Their calls are a reminder that it's time to order sunflower seeds—although it isn't necessary for the jays, who manage very nicely on the acorns and beechnuts that are plentiful in our neighborhood.

Even so, they protest vehemently if they find that the feeder is not stocked.

Without the jays and their equally noisy relatives, the crows, who sometimes congregate in our woods, these autumn days would be very quiet. It is not a time for birdsong. Most of the summer residents have departed without a word, and the migrants that are passing through are mainly silent. Having no need to sing to attract a mate or establish their territory, they don't waste energy in outpourings of song.

So it came as a surprise to me, on a quiet Indian summer morning, to hear a prolonged, melodious song that was strange and unknown. I was enjoying a cup of coffee and the morning paper on the screened porch —possibly for the last time of the season—when the soft, gentle warble penetrated my consciousness. It had the quality of a love song or a lullaby.

Looking around for the unknown singer, I was amazed to find that it was a bluejay, perched in a shrub on the other side of the screen, close enough to be reading the paper over my shoulder. He seemed oblivious to my presence—and he was definitely not singing a love song or a lullaby. There were no young ones in sight, nor a mate to be serenaded. He was all alone, and he was hunched down in a peculiarly contemplative pose, his crest flattened, his head tucked in and turned slightly to one side.

I sat motionless while he continued to sing the gentle, muted melody all to himself. It was as if he had grown weary of the arduous activities of the summer—the courting, and nesting, and tending the young—and now, his work done, he could settle down for a moment of peaceful reflection.

We usually see the cocky egomaniac, shouting his own name endlessly; the gangster, running with the mob; the alarmist, calling out warnings when a cat or a hawk is lurking about; the terrorist, chasing all competitors from the feeding station, intimidating smaller birds. And worse.

It was almost embarrassing to catch this brash, noisy fellow in an unguarded moment when he had stepped out of character, revealing a facet of his personality that we seldom see.

Everyone has tales to tell about the mean jays. Like the mild-mannered farm woman who flashed pure hatred when she heard their cries.

"Bluejays!" she exclaimed, as if announcing a barbarian invasion. "I kill 'em! I kill 'em every chance I get!"

I didn't ask what method she used to dispatch them, but I believed her. She spoke as if she were performing a patriotic duty. She had her reasons.

"I've seen 'em steal eggs out of my cardinals' nest and I've seen 'em kill baby robins. They'll even kill baby chickens."

I had never seen any of those things, but there are reports too numerous and reliable to deny. The bluejay has predatory habits, and people who divide the bird world into good guys and bad guys can find easy justification for killing bluejays. The can even find legal sanction; jays do not merit the protection of federal laws that prohibit the killing of most songbirds.

The trouble is, most people don't think of the bluejay as a songbird. Few have had the privilege of hearing his rare, whispered song. I have heard it only once. But I have never heard a mockingbird that could rival that haunting October song.

Command Decision

NOW AND THEN MY BRAIN GETS STUCK ON A HALF-remembered poem about the Emperor Charles of Spain who, with "his swarthy, grave commanders," was engaged in a campaign against "a frontier town of Flanders." From that point I lose exact words and rhymes, but I remember the narrative.

During the siege, a swallow built a nest in the emperor's tent and was still brooding when the battle was won and tents were being struck to move on. It was then that Charles proved himself a true friend of swallows. In a dramatic gesture, he sacrificed his tent, with the curt order to his men: "Leave it standing."

This story, as told by Longfellow, comes back to me when I hear current examples of human plans being altered for the welfare of birds. I thought of it when my sister halted construction on a wing of her new house. Like the Emperor Charles, she was protecting the nest of a swallow.

In the same spirit, though on a lesser scale, a friend of mine abandoned her decision to install an air conditioner in her bedroom when she found a mourning dove nesting on the window sill. And a neighbor postponed his house painting because he did not want to disturb the bluejays that had taken up residence in a shrub that nestled close to the house.

It is remarkable that birds can take decisions right out of our hands.

Take, for example, our problem of removing the mimosa tree that grew up in our back yard as a weed. Of course we should have pulled it up while it was still weed-size. But it was rather pretty and fern-like and doing no harm in the flowerbed at the edge of the patio. So we procrastinated.

By autumn it had become a small sapling, too big to be pulled up by the roots. We determined to cut it down. But there was no hurry. That was a job that could wait till spring.

Meanwhile, during the winter months, cardinals and bluejays brightened its bare boughs. We could look down on them from the living room window and watch them use the tree as a springboard to the nearby feeding platform. We scattered seeds on the ground under the tree for the juncos and white-throated sparrows that perched in it on snowy days. Later in the season we hung an extra feeder from one of the stronger branches to please the titmice and chickadees. It would come down in the spring when we cut down the tree.

With spring came a season of rapid growth—and of compromise. We pruned the ambitious branches heavily, but we let the tree stand. A flock of goldfinches, in a salute to our indecision, transformed the mimosa into a bright daffodil tree . . . and another season passed.

We watched the leafy branches spread, casting an unwelcome shadow on our sun-starved herbs, and wondered if by repeated prunings we could produce a miniature mimosa, a sort of bonsai version. It seemed unlikely.

By autumn, we would have to make the hard decision.

In the hot days of August we kept the sprinklers on in the back yard for an hour or so each day. Whole families of birds—cardinals, song sparrows, titmice, and chickadees—came to enjoy daily showers. One 98-degree afternoon, from my air-conditioned vantage point I watched a flock of chickadees *bathing* in the mimosa. Spreading their wings, they wallowed luxuriously in the drops of water that clung to the leaves. The clever ones discovered that they could enjoy a bath and a shower at the same time by positioning themselves underneath a dripping leaflet.

It was a lively scene, with six chickadees splashing and fluttering in the best bird bath we could ever have provided them.

Once more we wavered in indecision. How could we deprive them, or ourselves, of such pleasure?

Still, the tree was poorly placed—not where we would have chosen to plant a mimosa, even if we had selected a mimosa for our grounds in the first place. And it was getting much too big for the space.

Decision time was closing in on us. And then on an Indian summer day when the migration was in full swing, an American redstart stopped in to rest and found the mimosa to his liking. It made a perfect background for his vivid orange-and-black coloring, and I spent as much time as I could steal from a busy day watching his flashy performance as he flitted about, fanning out his two-colored tail, pausing now and then to savor an insect.

The redstart was the first of a wave that brought an astounding variety of warblers to the tree: magnolias, parulas, a chestnut-sided, bay-breasted, a black-throated green.

Innocently unaware, they were casting a bloc vote against our shaky decision. Oh, we'll talk of it again, I'm sure, as autumn edges into winter, and we may even steel ourselves to do some radical pruning. But in honor of the birds it has brought into our view, and in anticipation of all the others that will come with the passing seasons, we can really make only one reasonable decision about the troublesome mimosa:

"Leave it standing."

The Hungry Bird's Diet

BEYOND MY KITCHEN WINDOW IS A THRIVING PYRACANTHA, and in that pyrancantha one morning in early October I saw a black-throated blue warbler—the first one to visit our property, as far as I know, and a very welcome sight.

He was a handsome adult male, his black-and-blue-and-white plumage as bright and fresh as in springtime. I caught the flicker of his white wing-patch as he moved silently about in the foliage. No "confusing fall warbler," he.

But yes, on second look, he *was* confusing, or perhaps confused. Added to his black, blue, and white coloring was one small artistic touch of brilliant red.

As a ray of sun spotlighted him, I saw he was holding a pyracantha berry in his beak, as if in imitation of a cardinal. He rolled it over on his tongue, then gulped it down and went for more, while I pondered on the unusual sight of a berry-eating warbler.

He spent the whole day in that same bush, alternately

resting and browsing. Occasionally he would drop down to pick up his traditional fare of spiders and small insects near the ground; then he would work his way up again to feed on the clustered berries.

Next morning he was gone, and I concluded that birds in migration will change their feeding habits considerably in order to fuel up for the long journey.

At spring migration time I had seen a flock of white-throated sparrows forsake their seed-eating habits to take advantage of an early-season feast of insects swarming low over the ground. They behaved like fly-catchers, leaping into the air, fluttering and hovering to catch the insects on the wing.

Other birds, too, adopt flycatcher tactics when appetite and opportunity coincide. Cedar waxwings, who thrive on fruit and berries, can be adept at capturing flying insects, and even house sparrows will occasionally zoom through the air in pursuit of an attractive moth.

I once saw a pileated woodpecker go through a series of incredible aerial maneuvers in what turned out to be a futile effort to catch a cicada, and only a few days before the visit of the black-throated blue warbler, I had watched a grackle put on a similar show, executing loops, dives, and side-slips above the treetops in a manner uncharacteristic of his usual military dignity.

I thought he had taken leave of his senses, but when I put my binoculars on him I discovered that he was being led by a darting insect of considerable size—most likely a cicada—that would have made a hefty meal. Pursued and pursuer disappeared behind the trees, so I never saw who won, but I wouldn't have put any bets on the grackle. He had spent too many hours in straight-line flying to be an effective flycatcher.

When I think of characteristic feeding habits, I always recall The Day of the Kestrels at Cape May. That, too, was a day in early October, and kestrels began coming over in great numbers at nine o'clock in the morning.

At mid-afternoon they were still coming in steadily.

I stood on a slight elevation watching them fan out over a weedy field to feed. There were thirty of them, evenly spaced, hovering and diving by turns. It occurred to me suddenly that although they dove frequently into the tall weeds, obviously for food, they never alighted. Were they all missing their prey?

I couldn't understand it. But again, the binoculars gave me the answer. The prey, I soon discovered, were grasshoppers, which were both large and abundant, and the kestrels were so ravenous they were actually eating on the run. Focusing on one bird, I followed him as he hovered, dropped down, and came up with a fat grasshopper clutched in his talons. Then he continued to hover, bending his head forward to feed on his fresh catch. Even as he devoured the grasshopper, his eye was roving over the field in search of more.

His fellow travelers were all using the same strategy with remarkable efficiency. It was new to me, but obviously not to them. They continued feeding in that manner for more than an hour, during which time not one of them stopped to rest.

It was a beautiful demonstration of how hungry migrants can adapt to get necessary nourishment in their brief stopovers.

But it is not always the conditions of migration that prompt a change in eating patterns. Sometimes it is a matter of necessity. Robins that choose to spend the winter with us (and a surprising number of them do) haven't a chance of finding worms in the frozen ground, so they subsist on winter berries. But when the supply runs low in the waning days of winter, they must make other choices. I have seen them congregate in pine trees for shelter and tear pine cones apart for seeds.

A northern harrier, or marsh hawk, driven to desperation when heavy snows made rodent hunting impossible, learned to eat fish instead. A group of us standing on the bank of the Potomac looking for ducks among the floating ice masses watched in amazement as the hawk hovered over the water in osprey fashion and plunged down to spear a dead fish floating on the surface. He lacked the osprey's skill and precision, but motivation more than compensated.

Sometimes birds, not in dire straits at all, seem to be driven by mere whim. So it appeared to me one summer day when I was watching a flock of cattle egrets. They were mingling, typically, with a herd of cattle that was resting and ruminating.

Some of the egrets were strolling about, others were perched on the backs of patient cattle, and all were feeding contentedly. The supply of insects seemed to be abundant, and there was no quarreling over territory.

But one of the egrets wandered restlessly away from the main scene and headed toward a nearby pond. And there on the bank he encountered an unsuspecting frog basking in the ooze of mud, all safe and secure in the presence of the insectivorous egret.

That was his last bask. One snap and he was in the grip of a beak that was designed for much smaller prey. It was a struggle for both egret and frog—a struggle that lasted fully five minutes before the venturesome gourmet was able to position the frog lengthwise and swallow it.

Looking at the uncomfortable bulge on the bird's slender neck, I wondered if this was his first and last frog meal, or only the first of many.

Gifts from an Ill Wind

THE GUSTY NORTHWEST WIND THAT HAD WAKENED ME IN the night brought a clear, sunny day and a sharp temperature drop. It also brought a ruby-crowned kinglet to my bedroom window.

Before I was fully awake, I was up and running for binoculars to verify my blurry-eyed identification. He was the first kinglet of the season, possibly the same one that had stayed with us for a week in April, a pert little bird with white bars on his greenish wings and an exaggerated white eye-ring that gave him an expression of perpetual surprise.

A day that begins with a ruby-crowned kinglet offers little room for complaint. But to a birder, as a friend of mine once observed, the absence of birds is as significant as their presence, and even as I followed the pirouettes of the energetic little kinglet, I was remarking on the absence of thrushes.

It had been a full month since I had seen either the wood thrush or the veery that spend their summers with us. But by mid-October it was time for the northern nesters to be coming through: the Swainson's, the hermit, and the rarer gray-cheeked thrush. In my walks along the towpath, I had seen dozens of the buffy-faced Swainson's and even a few gray-cheeks, but not a single one had appeared in our woods.

Their absence led me to muse on other species that we had never seen on our property at all, and to wonder why this should be. Over a decade we had counted eight-five species—a record that is envied by many friends who wonder why we should have better luck than they. They assume it is because we offer superior food, but this is not the secret. The majority of our visitors don't even come to the feeders. They may come to feed on our bugs and berries, or they may just find it a convenient resting place in their travels. Often their stops are brief—and if I see more species than my neighbors, it's probably because I spend more time staring out the window when I might be doing something more practical.

Yet for all my watchfulness, there were unexplained gaps in my backyard list. In the spirit of friendly rivalry that is common to birders, I compare notes with friends in similar suburban settings, and I could not help wondering why fox sparrows, for example, should pass up Melody Lane but visit the Hannays in Chevy Chase regularly every year. Or why the Mehlmans, only a mile away, should be visited by red-breasted nuthatches when our property attracts only the white-breasted variety.

Just as the thought of nuthatches passed through my brain, I spied one that had appeared, as if on cue, high up in the tulip poplar where the kinglet was browsing. He was making his way down the trunk head-first in typical nuthatch fashion.

White-breasted nuthatches live in our woods. I hear their nasal cries more often than I see them, but they are a common enough sight that I don't feel impelled to study them with binoculars. This one, however, looked so small and short of tail that it merited a closer look.

Incredibly, it turned out to be a red-breasted nuthatch.

He had undoubtedly come in on the same northwest wind that had brought the kinglet, but it was an eerie coincidence that he should appear at the very moment I was musing upon his absence.

No. 86 on my backyard list continued downward on the tree trunk to eye level, showing off his distinctive markings and his delicate coloration. Smaller than his white-breasted relative, he was also quicker in his movements. On a sudden whim, he flitted from the tulip tree and landed on the platform feeder in the middle of the yard. He found nothing there to his liking, but he perched there long enough to afford an even more satisfying view—and long enough to draw my gaze to another bird resting quietly in a low shrub just beyond the feeder.

I did not immediately recognize the inconspicuous gray-backed bird with its light belly and sprinkling of breast spots, but the binoculars revealed yet another of the birds on my "missing" list.

It was a gray-cheeked thrush, the first to visit our property, so far as I knew. (I always have to add that qualifying phrase. Who knows how many gray-cheeked thrushes have stopped here without being seen?)

It was only luck that I saw this one. Three minutes later he was up and gone after stopping briefly to examine the compost pile at the edge of the woods. I just happened to be at the window for those brief three minutes.

More contented with his findings, the red-breasted nuthatch stayed around all day. He worked silently, but it was easy to locate him whenever I took time to look out.

During my mid-morning coffee break, he put on a show that I had never seen before. It is common to see nuthatches climb up or down a tree trunk in spirals, but I had never seen one *fly* in spirals around a tree. This little fellow did it quite systematically. He started at the foot of a tulip tree and flew swiftly upward, circling close in to the trunk as if investigating it for promising spots to browse. After disappearing briefly among the upper branches, he dropped down to the foot of the next tree and scanned it in the same manner, like an efficient reader scanning a newspaper.

Next morning, he, too, was gone. No. 86 and No. 87 had checked in and out within twenty-four hours. But they raised my spirits as they raised my hopes. Surely, if I spend enough time at the window, the fox sparrow will eventually show up. Meanwhile, there is the faithful little kinglet to enjoy.

Between Two Worlds

ONE OF THE CHARMS OF WATCHING BIRDS IS THE DELIGHT-ful mingling of the expected and the unexpected.

For example, I can expect the yellow-bellied sapsucker to stop off each spring to revisit his old drill site in the deodar cedar, which I can monitor from the kitchen window. Year after year he returns, very satisfyingly on schedule the last week in March, and stays for a week before moving on.

How do I know it's the same bird? I don't—and only a banding project would prove it conclusively. But is it logical to assume that a total stranger would fly un-erringly to the same spot on the same tree at the same time each spring?

The Cape May warbler is also on my expected list. I can expect him to appear in the spruce tree on the north side of the house each spring. By May 14 or 15 at the latest, I can expect to hear the modest song announcing his arrival, just in time for breakfast. The excitement has not diminished over the years. I leave my coffee to get

Cape May Warbler

cold while I go out to greet the little wanderer, knowing I will find him in the same spruce tree and that he will hop out on its spire to sing his cheery song and display his fresh spring colors.

I can expect him to stay with us for a week or ten days, depending on weather, spending most of his time in that same spruce tree. He will move on to seek out a similar spruce for his nest up in New Brunswick or Nova Scotia.

Is it the same Cape May warbler, six springs in a row? Again, I have no proof, only the strong evidence of coincidence: same time, same yard, same tree.

I do *not* expect either the sapsucker or the Cape May warbler in my back yard during fall migration. Both species have appeared, unpredictably and irregularly, but usually for brief one-night stands, and I have never had any particular reason to believe that these were my regular springtime guests, returning by the same route. Nor have I had any reason to link the two together. What can a yellow-bellied sapsucker and a Cape May warbler have in common?

A great deal, as I learned one day last October when I was loitering over the kitchen sink and gazing out the window.

Something moved on the trunk of the deodar, and I realized it was a sapsucker (*the* sapsucker?) flattened against the maimed bark, which we had painted with a protective coat of creosote after his last destructive visit. Surely this was the same bird, quite at home and drilling vigorously at the same old site.

He disappeared, and I turned my attention elsewhere. Next time I chanced to look out, I saw a small bird flattened against the trunk of the deodar, spread-eagle fashion, just at the edge of the blackened scar. It clung to the bark like a nuthatch or a creeper, but it was neither of these.

I needed binoculars to convince me that this was a Cape May warbler, behaving in such a curious manner. Was it *my* Cape May warbler? I couldn't be sure, of course, but it was an adult male, and only a few yards away from the tree I've come to know (in spring) as the Cape May Spruce.

But what on earth was he doing? Clearly, he was drinking sap from the holes that had been drilled by the sapsucker.

The little migrant must be powerfully thirsty, I concluded. But this was not just a passing phenomenon. Again and again within the next three days, I watched the two birds taking turns at their drinking fountain. The sapsucker would do his drilling while the warbler waited politely on a nearby branch. Then as soon as the sapsucker yielded his place, the warbler moved in and took his turn.

The performance baffled me considerably until I men-

tioned it to a friend who had just read an article about
our summer birds and how they adapt to conditions in
the tropics where they spend the winter.

"He's in training!" she exclaimed. "He's practicing up
for his winter diet!"

She explained that the Cape May warbler, like many
of our summer residents, changes its eating habits completely on its winter feeding grounds. The Cape May
warbler we know lives primarily on insects; the Cape
May warbler known in the West Indies is a nectar sipper,
getting his sustenance from fruits that he punctures with
his beak. He even has a hollow tongue, especially adapted
for sipping fruit juice—as easy as sucking through a
straw. It was this convenience that made it possible for
him to share the sapsucker's treasure.

Fascinated with this new knowledge, I began reading
more about Cape May warblers. Griscom and Sprunt,
in *The Warblers of North America*, published in 1957, described them as "generally insectivorous, but known to
do damage to vineyard grapes in fall migration." Earlier,
Bent's *Life Histories of North American Warblers* had quoted
several reports of Cape Mays "feeding on (or drinking
from) ripening grapes . . . one of the few instances of
warblers departing from an insect diet."

Now, in these days of easy travel and worldwide birding, we have the benefit of reports from observers who
have seen how our familiar birds adjust in different habitats. I turned to an article by Roger F. Pasquier ("Whose
Birds Are They?") in *The Nature Conservancy News* (July/
August 1982) to learn more about "my" Cape May warbler. After a summer in the spacious spruce forests of
Canada, where insects are abundant and the competition for them is minimal, he goes to his tropical winter
quarters, where he must compete with nineteen other
warbler species, in a season when insects are relatively
scarce. So he survives by changing to a fruit juice and
nectar diet.

It gave me a small touch of pride to read this of my

annual visitor: "Unique in its family, the Cape May warbler has evolved a tubular tongue that enables it to exploit these food sources more efficiently than its relatives."

This spring, the expected and the unexpected jumbled together in a curious way.

The yellow-bellied sapsucker did not put in an appearance. One cannot take too much for granted.

The Cape May warbler interrupted my breakfast on May 4, a full ten days ahead of schedule. I left my coffee and went out to greet him with new appreciation, knowing him better than I did a year ago. I can trace his route on the map. I know all about his double life, his remarkable adaptation to the conditions he encounters in his travels.

Unique in his family. And he has chosen my back yard as a way station between his two worlds!

PART FOUR
Troublesome Birds . . .

Birds Can Be Pests

On a trip through Loveland, Colorado, several years ago, we stopped at a roadside Chamber of Commerce booth where two young high school girls were dispensing maps and information. They greeted us cordially, offered assistance, and asked what we were interested in seeing.

"Birds," we replied promptly.

We were unprepared for the looks of consternation that crossed their faces at that one word.

"Oh, yes!" one of the girls exclaimed. "We've had a *terrible* time with birds around here!"

Apparently we had arrived in the wake of a blackbird plague that was not soon to be forgotten by Lovelanders.

For those of us who find our major pleasure in the pursuit and observation of birds, it is difficult to think of them as someone else's major problem. But there are reminders, from time to time, that birds can be pests—even menaces.

Some of our worst air disasters have been caused by

birds whose flyways conflicted with those of the commercial airlines. And the great flocks of blackbirds that congregate in residential communities on their migration route can present a real health hazard to humans if they stay too long.

But even individual birds can wear out their welcome.

In the days of early spring, I am frequently summoned to the telephone to help some frantic homeowner solve the problem of a destructive woodpecker. It is usually the smallest, least offensive of the species, the little downy woodpecker, who is attacking the siding of a house, drilling unsightly holes and making a racket that is unbelievable for his size. Sometimes a red-bellied woodpecker, twice the size of the downy, goes berserk and becomes a nuisance.

Both may be difficult to discourage, but many people have found that the birds can be frightened away by a fluttering object hanging near the drill site, or by a piece of shiny metal such as a coffee-can lid nailed over the hole.

But there are exceptions.

I recall the frantic young mother who called for help when a persistent red-bellied woodpecker was attacking her house in the early hours of morning, waking the children with his noise and frightening them half to death. Her husband had threatened to shoot it, which appalled her—but she was clearly near the end of her rope.

I gave her the shiny-metal suggestion and there was a long pause. I wondered if we'd been disconnected.

"It's a shiny piece of metal he's banging on," she said at last, and I could hear desperation in her voice.

The red-belly had discovered a metal ventilator pipe on the roof of the new house, and he began beating on it as soon as the sun struck it in the morning. The sound of that clanging echoing through the house was enough to wake anyone from a deep sleep, and enough to make the children cry in terror.

The parents were almost equally terrified at first, thinking that the noise was in the plumbing and must be caused by a faulty water heater that could explode any minute. It was only by chance that they discovered the woodpecker up on the roof and identified the source of the din. Their momentary relief gave way to annoyance and then to desperation as the bird continued his dawn attacks, day after day.

And here I was, advising shiny metal as a deterrent.

It was not as idiotic as it sounded, I assured her. The idea of the shiny metal is to give the bothersome bird a glimpse of his own reflection, which he may mistake for a competitor claiming his territory. Her resident red-belly was undoubtedly seeing his reflection in the side of the ventilator pipe, but rather than being intimidated by the competition, he was attacking it vigorously.

In that case, the thing to do was to paint his rival right out of the picture. I advised my caller to send her husband up on the roof, armed—not with a shotgun, but with a can of spray paint.

Hope returned to her voice, and she promised to call me if the experiment was unsuccessful so that we could explore alternative solutions. I have not heard from her since, so I assume that her problem, as well as the woodpecker's, was solved by that simple device. I hope her children are sleeping serenely through the early morning hours, and that the confused red-belly has turned his attention to peaceful pursuits.

Sapsuckers Outstay Their Welcome

OF THE TREES ON OUR PROPERTY, THE DEODAR CEDAR IS the most prized. It is a beautiful specimen in all seasons and attracts a variety of wildlife, ranging from raccoons to kinglets, and it brings all these within view of the kitchen window.

It was from this vantage point one March morning that I spotted a yellow-bellied sapsucker hammering industriously on the main trunk. Since sapsuckers stop here only briefly and infrequently in spring and fall, it was worth delaying breakfast to pay attention.

The bird was rather oddly marked, with mottled black-and-white front and back, and the longitudinal white wingstripe characteristic of the species was barely discernible. It had an unusually large red cap, boldly outlined in black. With a turn of the head, it showed a white throat, identifying it as a female.

She spent most of the day in the same location. Next morning, flying conditions were unfavorable, and she stayed on the job all day in the drenching rain. By the third day she seemed so attached to the spot that even fair weather and a southeasterly breeze could not induce her to move on.

In the bright sunlight of that morning, I could observe the work she had done on the preceding day, when heavy rain had reduced visibility. What I saw concerned me. She was not drilling the usual neat parallel rows of small holes that I had seen so many times, especially on fruit trees. She had outlined a long rectangle, about two by five inches, and was systematically ripping off strips of bark between the holes.

The rectangle grew larger as the day advanced. From time to time the driller disappeared for a half-hour or so, and during her absence other birds visited the drill site and partook of the oozing sap. Carolina chickadees, who had been inspecting the wren house hung from a lower branch of the deodar, watched for opportunities to sneak a sip, and a squirrel took advantage of the sapsucker's absence to get a drink, then flattened his body over the elongated scar as if to take possession. But the next time I looked, the sapsucker had reclaimed her territory and was working as energetically as before.

But something was different. The bird's coloring was bolder, its wingstripe more sharply defined. When it turned its head, it revealed a bright crimson throat. This was the male.

So we were entertaining a pair of yellow-bellied sapsuckers—the first time we had ever been so honored.

It soon became doubtful that the two were a pair, or even traveling companions, for they never appeared together. Five days passed before we saw the female again, and just as we had concluded that she had gone on her way alone, there she was at seven o'clock in the morning, exactly a week after her first appearance.

Meanwhile, the male had made great progress, enlarging the drilled area to a sizable triangle that looked like a huge claw mark inflicted by a grizzly bear. His devotion to duty reached the level of obsession. With only short breaks through the day, he was there from dawn's early light until dark. For all we knew, he stayed on duty through the night.

Indoors, we had not been idle. The bizarre sapsucker behavior had prompted a search of the literature to determine whether it could actually be detrimental to the tree. One authority after another assured us that sapsuckers do no harm to trees but can be credited with saving whole orchards by ridding them of insidious borers.

But at last we found an authority who struck a warning note, confirming our fears for our favorite tree. Edward Howe Forbush, in *A Natural History of American Birds*, noted that "most of the trees marked by the sapsucker's characteristic pits seem not to be injured thereby," then added ominously:

> But there is another kind of sapsucker work where the bird pecks out larger holes, often roughly rectangular or triangular in shape. In some cases the bird so injures the bark over large areas that the remaining bark between the holes dries out, and if these punctured areas extend entirely around the trunk, the tree is girdled and it dies.

Forbush, too, must have observed obsessed sapsuckers at work, for he concluded:

> If an individual once gets the habit of visiting a favorite tree, it continues to visit it until the tree either dies or becomes so enfeebled that the bird prefers some more vigorous subject.

That was the clincher. Before the female returned we had already launched Operation Discouragement, and we had already learned how difficult it is to discourage a male sapsucker. The female was just as resistant. We took turns standing under the tree, clapping hands, shouting, banging pot lids together, and even heaving rocks in her general direction.

The only effect was to make her move to the other side of the trunk where she would "hide," peering out occasionally to see if the coast was clear. Only rarely did she fly off to observe her enemies from a nearby spruce.

Time was on her side—time and the chickadees. Having nothing else pressing for her attention, she could outwait and outwit us. And the chickadees, who had begun nesting in the wren house, became so agitated by our commotion that we were forced to desist for fear of losing them as close neighbors.

There was one encouraging thought: The sapsuckers couldn't stay forever. They would have to move north to their nesting area sooner or later. We hoped, as we watched the growing gash on the deodar, that it would be sooner. Never before had we been eager to speed a migrant on its way.

We called the Department of Agriculture for suggestions. A tree expert (clearly no bird lover) expressed regret that there was no chemical known to deter marauding sapsuckers, but he recommended treating the scar with tree-wound dressing and then covering it with protective wire mesh.

By the time we had assembled the necessary materials, including an extension ladder, the female sapsucker had been replaced by the male, who was even more recalcitrant than she, staring boldly down at us as we set the ladder in place and even posing for pictures alongside his handiwork.

Deciding that the pictures would be better lighted by the morning sun, and that the sapsucker could scarcely inflict lethal damage on the tree overnight, we left the ladder in position ready for the next day's operations.

That ladder must have served as handwriting on the sapsucker's wall. With mingled relief and regret, we discovered that he was not on the job at the customary hour next morning. We did not see him—or her—again.

The chickadees continued serenely with the nesting project. From the kitchen window we could watch their trips to and from the little house that was meant for wrens, directly beneath the glistening black patch of tree-wound dressing left as a lasting souvenir of the sapsuckers' extended visit.

Avian Davids vs. Goliaths

GOOD NEWS IS HARD TO COME BY THESE DAYS, SO IT GIVES me special pleasure to pass the word that our mockingbirds, after a mysterious and prolonged absence, are back with us.

That isn't quite accurate. Actually, they are not *our* mockingbirds. They belong to no one, and they make this clear to anyone who will stop and listen to their unmistakable declarations of independence. And I should not say that they are "back." Clearly, this is not the same pair that accepted our hospitality for six years and then mysteriously disappeared last November.

These are newcomers. They don't even know where to apply for raisin rations. But they do know how to make life miserable for the neighborhood cats, and for all the dogs that venture onto our property with no good intentions in mind. I'm grateful for that. The lawn-mowing chore is more pleasant when there is a mockingbird on duty to police the dogs—and to sing of his victories. I get protection and entertainment at the same time, and so far without the disbursement of a single raisin.

Of course the time may come, as I know only too well, when I will be under attack myself. Mockingbirds have no delusions about property ownership. They are fierce defenders of *their* territory, especially during the mating season, and have been known to tackle imagined adversaries much more formidable than I.

Even less aggressive birds show remarkable temerity during the nesting season. A house wren will turn on a robin or a bluejay in the blink of an eye, and I have seen a chickadee sail into a red-bellied woodpecker that happened to pick the wrong limb to explore for grubs. The surprised woodpecker retreated to another corner of the woods, with the chickadee in hot pursuit.

Anyone who takes time to scan the summer sky will soon observe that the common sight is not that of large birds intimidating small birds, but of small birds harassing larger ones that may or may not pose a threat. Even the nonpredatory turkey vultures, which feed exclusively on carrion, are subject to attack. In fact, a turkey vulture was the prime target in one of the most unusual chase scenes I have witnessed, involving three different species of varying sizes. The bird in the middle was a crow. He was making repeated assaults on the vulture and simultaneously fending off a heckling grackle.

It is much more common to see crows gang up on a hawk twice their size, and it is equally common to see a crow defending himself against relentless attacks by grackles or red-winged blackbirds. These attacks are not without reason, it must be admitted. Sometimes if you follow closely with your binoculars as a persistent red-wing dive-bombs a crow in flight, you may see the crow drop the egg he has stolen from the red-wing's nest.

But red-wings are not always so rational in identifying The Enemy. A great blue heron, huge as he is by comparison, is not a threat to a red-winged blackbird. But

I have seen an innocent heron that made the mistake of fishing too close to a red-wing's nest forced to move to another pond under repeated assault by the angry red-wing.

The sight of this majestic bird with his nearly-six-foot wingspan being intimidated by a relative midget defies one's sense of proportion and arouses mingled feelings of sympathy for the pursued and admiration for the plucky pursuer, however misguided he may be. The only comparable deed I have witnessed in the bird world was that of a hummingbird's diving directly onto the back of a sharp-shinned hawk in mid-air.

I have no idea what prompted the attack. It was past the nesting season, and there was no evidence that the sharp-shin, with his attention turned to migration, had done anything to harm the hummingbird (although he could have made a quick meal of his attacker). Who knows? The brash little bird may have been settling an old score, or maybe he was practicing deterrent aggression. Fortunately, it did not prove to be a kamikaze attack.

From what I have observed, birds have some trouble in sorting out friends and foes. So I will be startled but not surprised if the new mockingbird suddenly descends, screaming, upon my head as I work in the garden. It's his job to keep his little world safe from monsters like me.

Nobody Loves the Cowbird

"YOU'LL NEVER BELIEVE THIS BIRD I'VE GOT ON MY FEEDER," said the voice on the phone. "It has a dark blue body, and its head is all brown."

I believed it. The brown-headed cowbird is common enough in our area, and although the male is usually described as black, his shiny feathers often appear to be midnight blue.

My caller couldn't believe that this was a rather ordinary bird she was seeing. "I've never seen such a bird before," she insisted.

But she probably had seen many cowbirds without recognizing them, flying overhead with the mixed flocks of grackles, starlings, and red-winged blackbirds with which they travel. The expert eye can pick them out by their size. They are the smallest of the "blackbirds," and the least admired.

The female cowbird, blatantly promiscuous and totally lacking in maternal instinct, provides moralists with a perfect example of irresponsible motherhood. School-

children of my generation learned the cowbird's reputation through a poem (most probably written by a
Conscientious Mother of Five) that extolled the virtues
of the robin, the bluebird, and other domestic types and
then disclosed the scandal of "that lazy, mean bird—
the cowbird, so bold and so daring":

Too lazy to build, she just lays her eggs
In other birds' nests, never caring.

Of course, it's true. At least it's true that the cowbird
leaves her eggs in the nests of other birds: mourning
doves, sparrows, warblers, vireos. She is not particular
about whose nest it is. But this does not necessarily
demonstrate either "laziness" or "meanness." Her behavior is part of her genetic endowment, and it has
nothing to do with morality or weakness of character.

Because the ancestors of our present-day cowbirds
traveled with roaming buffaloes, feeding on insects that
were attracted to the herds, they developed a nomadic
lifestyle. They went where the food was. Mobility was
the key to their survival.

There was no provision for maternity leave. So the
female cowbird—more resourceful than lazy—solved
the problem by leaving her eggs and her parental responsibilities behind.

The modern cowbird follows the same pattern for the
best of all possible reasons: It works. In the spring you
will see her lurking around, eyeing the nesting birds
and staking out likely places to deposit her own eggs.

She distributes her favors indiscriminately, sometimes leaving only one egg in a nest, sometimes visiting
the same nest day after day until her entire clutch is
laid, and frequently throwing out the eggs of the nest's
rightful owner.

And so, as our moralizing poet concluded:

The other bird-mothers must bring up the young,
And care for the big cowbird babies.
While their mothers go dashing and flitting about
Like carefree society ladies.

The female cowbird, in her drab gray-brown dress, hardly fits the picture of the social butterfly, but compared with other birds she does appear to lead a fairly carefree life, unencumbered by family ties or housekeeping chores.

She mates only for the moment, with no need to be choosy; no burden of fatherhood will fall on the courting male. He, too, is free to go on his way, while the unwitting "foster parents" bring up the cowbird babies— most often at the expense of their own brood.

I have watched an exhausted little song sparrow following anxiously after a fat young cowbird twice her size, patiently stuffing food into its gaping mouth.

Chances are that this was the only survivor from her nest. In all probability her legitimate offspring were either pushed or crowded out of the nest by the cowbird, which, being bigger and more aggressive, got more than its share of the food.

Many small birds starve when the nest is dominated by a foundling cowbird.

In Michigan, where the rare Kirtland's warbler nests, the cowbird represents a real threat to the survival of the species, which is on the endangered list. Here, man has intervened and taken steps to control the cowbird population in this limited area.

Some birds have designed ingenious ways of outwitting the wily cowbird. Among the brighter ones is the little yellow warbler. Finding one of the speckled cowbird eggs in her nest, she builds another nest on top of it, sealing off the unwanted egg, even if she has to sacrifice one of her own eggs in the process. Where the cowbird is persistent, this may result in a two- or three-story nest, each story built above one or more cowbird eggs. There is at least one record of a yellow warbler nest six stories high.

Other birds have been known to break the cowbird egg, and still others may desert the nest, especially if it holds more than one of the alien eggs.

But most of them accept this unsought responsibility and play out their traditional role as parents, even when their own brood is lost. Our poet might find a Mother's Day message in all this, but the system works well for the cowbird. Lazy or not, it is unlikely to find a place on the endangered species list.

A Mockingbird
in a Crabtree

OUTSIDE, I HEAR THE UNPLEASANT SQUALL OF A MOCKING-bird—our mockingbird, we call him, since he has declared that our territory is his territory. But his squall is the same as that of any other possessive mockingbird, the same as the one that laid claim to the Supreme Court when I was working on Capitol Hill.

I used to hear that nasty squall each day when I passed by the Court on my way to lunch. It was uttered from the top of the flagpole where the mockingbird played King of the Hill.

He sang from that perch, too, often enough to be credited with redeeming social qualities. But he seemed to spend disproportionate time throwing out his harsh challenge to all who dared pass by on the public sidewalk.

He sometimes interrupted a magnificent aria to give that warning cry before plummeting downward in an aerial attack on an innocent pedestrian. Bipeds and quadrupeds alike were objects of his aggression. One day an amiable little mongrel was subjected to an assault that was so vicious and unrelenting that the poor bewildered beast chose the lesser of two evils and dove into a thorny hedge for cover. And there he stayed, cowering, while his attacker returned to the top of the flagpole and sang in utter tranquility.

It was not the nesting season, so the dog was not endangering a family. He was certainly not going to steal any berries from the hedge. So it was hard to imagine just what the Supreme Court tyrant was protecting.

There is no mystery about our own mockingbird's behavior. When I hear that squall, I know that he is protecting his crabtree. He laid claim to it early in the autumn and did battle with a rival mockingbird for all the rights and privileges.

From the kitchen window I watched the engagement, not recognizing it, at first, for combat. It started with the two birds facing off, less than a foot apart, on a utility wire, with feints and pirouettes that could easily have been mistaken for a high-wire mating dance of exquisite grace and precision.

But it was the off season for courtship, and the hostility underlying the performance became more and more evident as the two vied for feeding territory. The street was apparently the dividing line, and "our" bird skillfully held the line, forcing his opponent back into the woods beyond our neighbor's house.

Triumphantly, he took up his post atop the ornamental crabtree, with its abundant clusters of miniature fruit, just the right bite-size for mockingbirds.

The fruit is bite-size, too, for cedar waxwings, and in some years when no mockingbird has chosen to defend the tree, they have appeared in great numbers to strip it of every last morsel.

I wondered if the determined mockingbird could intimidate fifty or a hundred voracious waxwings. I hoped not. No matter how great their numbers or how hearty their appetites, cedar waxwings occupy Most Favored

Visitor status here, and it would disturb me to see them routed by an inhospitable mockingbird.

But with the advance of winter, I have seen my question answered. I have heard that resounding squall, and I have seen the Defender of the Tree take on a persistent flock of hungry starlings, numbering at least a hundred. They, too, find the crabapples bite-size and attractive, and they descend on the tree with a flurry that would overwhelm lesser spirits. But not our bird.

In the beginning, we were allies, he and I, in defending the tree. Whenever I saw the starling horde descend, I would fling open the window and shriek in proper fishwife style, waving my arms wildly to scare them off. But I soon learned that my efforts were superfluous.

Now when I see an onslaught of starlings, I stand back and watch the cool solo performance of our mockingbird. Appearing from nowhere, he gives a single war cry and sails into the flock like a sheepdog scattering a herd. The starlings retreat in utter confusion, and the victor takes his proud stand on the topmost branch of the tree, swallows two crabapples in rapid succession by way of celebration, and waits.

Starlings or cedar waxwings, what difference is it to him? When I hear that angry squall, I know that a flock of a thousand waxwings wouldn't have a chance.

"I Loved Him in the Spring . . ."

AGGRESSION IS HARD TO ESCAPE THESE DAYS. EVEN THE backyard, which looks so serene in the new snow, is a battleground.

We have provided an abundance of food and drink for all comers; and here, of all places, peace should reign. But an overly aggressive starling has taken over the suet feeder. It is big enough for several birds to share, but he wants it all to himself.

He snaps a menacing beak at the timid little downy woodpecker that backs down the tree and peers cautiously around the trunk to see if the coast is clear. She is easily intimidated by the surly starling and flies off to a nearby tree to wait her turn.

Her mate makes a circumspect approach to the feeder and suffers the same indignity. So does the larger, bolder hairy woodpecker that comes along minutes later. He should certainly be a match for the bully, but he doesn't even put up a fight.

Then comes the red-bellied woodpecker, a big, handsome fellow, his red cap glistening in the morning sunlight. Nothing circumspect about him. Forthright and direct, he flies straight to the suet and with one snap of his beak banishes the troublesome starling.

I feel like cheering.

The telephone rings and I leave the scene of the power struggle to commiserate with another feeder watcher who is having problems with an aggressive mockingbird.

"I don't know what's got into him," she complains. "I have feeders all over the back yard, and not a one of them is safe. He dive bombs all the birds that come near. He doesn't want the food himself; he just doesn't want *them* to have it. I don't have any purple finches left. What can I do with him?"

"I wish you could send him over to me," I reply honestly. There is a void in our yard just now. Our mockingbird has been missing for days, and I, who grew up in the midwest, where mockingbirds were unknown, now find them an indispensable part of my daily life. I hardly know how to start the day when there is no mockingbird at the window applying for his ration of raisins.

She assures me that I wouldn't want this one, and asks again, on a note of desperation, what she can do.

I offer the tactic that has worked for me in the past: I always dispensed raisins from a front window, on the opposite side of the house from the feeding stations, so there was never a conflict. Cardinals lurked around to pick up anything the mockingbird missed, but all the other birds kept to themselves, and the pampered mocker never invaded their territory.

My caller has already tried that ploy, without success. "I set up a special feeder for him in front of the house. He won't go near it, and the other birds won't go near it either. So it's just wasted."

I am not being very helpful.

"When I see all my little birds scared away," she goes

on, "I just get so mad at him! I loved him in the spring, but now—I'm ready to kill him!"

I make the mistake of laughing. Her complaint evokes memories of dogs, cats, even grown men, transformed into helpless, pitiful giants by merciless dive-bombing mockingbirds. And her reaction is so natural, so human. My laughter is not unsympathetic, but she misreads it.

"It's not funny!" she protests. "I'm serious. If I could catch him . . . "

She stops, and she relents.

"No, I could never really *hurt* a living thing," she admits. "But I *do* feel like wringing his neck sometimes."

Her words and tone give eloquent expression to the profound frustration we feel when a terrorist is at large and beyond anyone's control.

I have no advice to offer. I can only try to console this champion of justice and fair play.

"Maybe he'll wear himself out and get tired of his little game."

Maybe he will. Or maybe he'll get his comeuppance from another relentless aggressor. Like a starling, maybe —or a red-bellied woodpecker.

The Battered Bird Syndrome

AN EPIDEMIC OF WINDOW WASHING HERALDS THE ARRIVAL of spring. But people who take pride in their sparkling clear windows often invite problems. They may learn how distressing it is to hear the thud of a bird hitting the window and to find its limp body on the ground.

Sometimes the bird is only stunned and will revive in a half-hour or so if kept warm and quiet in a nice padded shoebox. The distraught home owner, feeling responsible for the accident, may not revive quite so quickly. And if the injured bird does not survive, the pangs of guilt persist.

I have had the experience only once, several years ago when a beautiful yellow-throated vireo crashed into our living room window and fell dead. Soon after that shattering episode, we hung a bright stained-glass cardinal in the window, suspended from a thin wire so that it swings gently, catching the sunlight and the attention of passing passerines. It has probably saved many a bird's life. The silhouette of a falcon, in the form of an inexpensive decal, placed strategically on the window, is just as effective, according to friends who have solved their window-kill problems with this device.

But there are other problems not so easily solved. Each spring I can anticipate a number of plaintive inquiries from anxious people who are coping with the battered bird syndrome.

"I have this crazy robin," the call is likely to begin, and I know at once that the crazy robin in pecking on a window, aggressively and obsessively. He has seen his reflection in the clean window and thinks that it is another robin competing for his territory.

The plaintiff is not interested in bird psychology. He, or she, just wants to know how to stop it, how to make the bird go away. The noise is bothersome.

I suggest closing the blinds. Usually this has already been tried and found useless. The bird just moves on to another window. Some birds seem to have a paranoid streak, finding an adversary in every window, and they will go to any lengths to eliminate it. Their attacks may be prolonged, but there is some consolation in knowing that this peculiar behavior is generally confined to the nesting season and will eventually subside.

"But I'm afraid she's going to kill herself!" one caller protested. "You wouldn't believe it. This bird is suicidal!"

The bird in question was a cardinal, and her attacks on the window were so determined and violent that both she and the window were smeared with blood. Time after time the conscientious housewife had shooed the bird away and washed the blood from the window, but obviously she couldn't devote her entire day to this one chore. And she was genuinely concerned for the life of the bird.

This was not the first time I had heard of a bird's mutilating itself, although I can find no records of self-destruction. Cardinals, both male and female, are especially prone to this kind of behavior. Robins run a close second, but other species, including even the gentle bluebirds, have been known to engage in "shadow box-

Cardinal

ing." Nor do they confine themselves to windows. Any shiny surface that offers a fairly clear reflection can become the object of an assault. A good clean hubcap can be a challenge to a nervous bird bent on defending its territory.

I once watched a northern oriole perched on a car's side mirror and doing battle with its reflection. This went on for perhaps twenty minutes until the owner returned to the parking lot and drove off. The agitated oriole promptly found another rival in another car mirror.

In all likelihood, the oriole's mate was sitting on a nest nearby while he went on his quixotic rounds, seeking to make the world safe for her and their brood. Their big mistake, of course, was in locating so near a parking lot with its aggregation of hubcaps and mirrors, which gave him a thousand enemies to fight off, single-beaked.

Mirrors placed near windows double the hazards in a house. One besieged home owner struggling over his income taxes was driven to distraction by an aggressive robin banging at his window. Analyzing the situation, he realized that the bird could see its reflection in the mirror hanging over his desk, at right angles to the window. He draped a towel over the mirror, and *voilà*, the problem was solved—at least for the taxpayer, if not for the robin, which may easily have found another rival elsewhere within his territory.

Within his territory—there's the clue. Birds will not range far afield searching out competitors, but they will assail any potential threat in their own domain. This is why battered bird reports always involve species that make their homes near human dwellings. It may not be a comfort to the harassed resident to know that the brave robin has a family nearby. "Like father, like son," they say, and who wants a whole new generation of masochistic window fighters? But this is not known to be a hereditary trait. Individual birds differ, and some are more aggressive in repelling competition, real or imagined.

Fortunately for the people who have to deal with the problem in their own homes, the period of siege is usually of short duration. While it lasts, it can be a subject of scientific observation.

Many years ago, the ornithologist Frank M. Chapman got a bright idea while watching a male cardinal fighting its reflection in a mirror. This might give him some information about the boundaries of the cardinal's territory. He did an experiment, moving the mirror around, farther and farther from the nest site. At one hundred yards, the cardinal still attacked it valiantly. But at 110 yards, the bird lost interest. The "rival" had been vanquished, forced out of his territory, and he was at peace.

My own conviction is that it is virtually impossible to discourage a bird with an obsession. But knowing that the bird is not likely to commit suicide, one can relax, observe, and take notes while waiting for the defender to declare a victory and withdraw from the field.

Eine Kleine Nachtmusik

MOST OF MY TELEPHONE CALLS COME FROM COMPLETE strangers. Someone has told them that I know about birds, so could I take just a minute . . . ?

Today it was a woman who was just wondering about all these birds she hears chirping at night.

It was some time past midnight when she woke to hear all these bird voices. She'd never heard such a thing before, and she thought something must be wrong. Aren't birds supposed to be asleep at night? I mean, you know, you cover a canary's cage at night so that he can get his rest. What kind of birds are these, and why are they awake at two o'clock in the morning?

I could answer only half of her question.

There was no doubt in my mind that "all those birds" were one mockingbird, going through his whole repertoire, sounding like a dozen different species. I could assure her that there was nothing wrong with him—that mockingbirds often sing on a moonlit summer night, sometimes for hours. But I couldn't tell her why.

Bird behaviorists have offered various theories for which there is no proof: His sleep cycle is out of synch. He is protecting his territory from nocturnal intruders. He is entertaining his brooding mate. And so on.

Still, there is no conclusive answer to the question "Why does the mockingbird sing at night?" The best answer I've heard is: "Why not?"

Another of my unknown callers (a weary lady with desperation in her voice) would be quick to tell you "why not." Because it disturbs her sleep, that's why not.

We had no problem with identification. She knew it was a mockingbird. She heard him often enough in the daytime, and that was okay. He just didn't know when to stop. She was bleary-eyed and edgy from loss of sleep, three nights in a row. (I noted that the moon was full, and the nights had been bright and clear.)

"He starts at one o'clock in the morning, right outside my window," she complained, "and he keeps it up until *five* A.M.! And then I have to get up and go to work. I can't go on. I don't want to kill him, but . . ."

But murder was in her heart, even though she knew the old saying that it's a crime to kill a mockingbird.

She had yelled at him, thrown things at him, but he sang on, blissfully undisturbed. A helpful friend had told her to call me for suggestions. What could she do to get rid of him?

It is uncomfortable to be cast as the last resort, especially when you can offer no help. All I could offer was sympathy and consolation. I had been through it myself, many times.

One summer, when I was at a low point, recovering much too slowly from surgery, a mockingbird chose the TV antenna just over my bedroom from which to sing his joyful nocturnal arias, beginning almost the minute I turned off the light and continuing well toward dawn. I stuffed cotton into my ears, pulled the pillow over my head, and turned on the bedside radio to drown him out. But in the end I decided that it was better just to

Mockingbird

listen, relax, and let my body heal. My time was not being wasted. If a bird could stay awake at night to sing so ecstatically, someone really should stay awake to listen.

I tried to impart a little of this to the frantic woman, and as the conversation continued I realized that I was sounding more like a sleep therapist than a bird expert.

"Have you tried ear plugs?"

"Yes, but I had to take them out because I was afraid I'd sleep through the alarm and be late for work."

"You could try going to bed a little earlier so that you'd have time to get into a sound sleep before the bird starts singing."

She sounded doubtful. "Don't you think it would wake me? He's *loud*, you know."

I knew. Loud, but beautiful.

"It isn't the kind of song you can ignore," she went on. "You have to listen to it. If he just repeated the same notes over and over, it would get monotonous and you'd fall asleep out of boredom. But it keeps changing. And it's so . . . *demanding*."

She had expressed it very well.

"It won't go on forever," I consoled her. "He does this only during the nesting season, so it will all be over by September. And pray for rain. That always keeps him quiet."

Meantime, my advice was and is: Relax and enjoy it. Don't try to sleep through it. Turn on the light and read. Nothing heavy; that wouldn't be compatible. Poetry is good. Something lyrical, like Wordsworth. Come to think of it, Walt Whitman's "Out of the Cradle Endlessly Rocking" would be perfect against a background of bird-song by night.

PART FIVE

. . . and Birds
in Trouble

A Life-and-Death Drama

IT WAS QUIET IN THE WOODS. THE MID-AFTERNOON HUSH warned us that we were not likely to see much birdlife at that hour, when migrant warblers and songbirds were resting. Later, around four o'clock, they would come to life and start taking on fuel for their night flight. But for now, they were out of sight.

It was siesta time, too, for summer residents preoccupied with the nesting season. A silent chickadee carrying a mouthful of food approached his nest by a devious route, but the secret of its location was revealed by the clamoring of the hungry babies. We could not see them, but we saw the patient parent perch on the edge of the nest with rations to distribute. The high-pitched voices silenced for the time being, the adult uttered a muted "Chick-a-dee-dee-dee" as an admonition or possibly a promise and went off to gather another offering.

In the distance a red-bellied woodpecker gave his harsh, gargling call, just once. Then a sleepy silence fell over the woods once again.

Enjoying the tranquility, we left the shaded path to

follow the stream that wound in and out of patches of sunlight that spotlighted buttercups and wild geraniums along its banks. As we progressed upstream, the banks became steeper, and the low murmur of the water gradually rose to an energetic babble as it splashed over the rocky bed.

Above the music of the water a steady, insistent "beep-beep-beep" captured out attention. We halted to listen. It sounded like a baby bird in distress.

Unable to determine the direction of the ventriloquial call, we continued on our way. Rounding a sharp bend in the stream, we came upon a tableau in the shadow of the overhanging bank opposite us. A female wood duck was floating there with her infant family clustered around her: eight fluffy ducklings out for their first swim.

This, then, was the source of the ceaseless beeping. The high, sharp note continued to sound at regular intervals as we watched. The sound, we realized, was not coming from the babies, but from their anxious mother.

It was clearly a signal. Was she warning them about us? Or about a more immediate danger, invisible to us from our vantage point?

We scanned the eroded bank with its tangle of roots, looking for signs of the predator—a snake, perhaps, or a raccoon—but we saw no cause for alarm. It was, in fact, a serene picture. In the cool shadows the mother had found a quiet pool formed by surrounding roots and rocks, a safe, secluded spot for a swimming lesson. But her alert pose and persistent alarm cry belied the tranquil appearance of the family group.

She saw us, but her eyes seemed to focus on a point downstream. There we discovered the cause of her distress.

Out in the main current where the water rushed downhill, creating a miniature rapids over the rocks, four more ducklings were treading water furiously, trying to catch up with the mother who continued to send out signals to them.

But they were fighting a losing battle. They were very

Wood Duck

young—probably only a day old—and the struggle was too much for them. In spite of their frantic efforts, the current was carrying them downstream toward a white-water hazard that no small duckling was likely to survive.

The mother's dilemma was poignant. With eight youngsters safely in tow and four in danger several yards away, what could she do?

Powerless to help, we watched the life-or-death drama unfold in this idyllic setting in the middle of a drowsy afternoon.

Instinctively, we drew back, fearing that our proximity was adding to her distress. From behind a thicket screen we watched in helpless fascination.

A sudden change in the shrill call note signaled a decision. On a lower tone, the mother seemed to be speaking to her tightly packed flock of eight. Then she climbed quickly over the heavy root that separated their safe haven from the turbulent mainstream.

Her difficult decision was made. She was leaving the larger group behind to go to the rescue of the endangered four.

But no—that was not the decision. The low command had not been "Wait here," but "Follow me." And the little ducks obeyed. One by one, they clambered over the root and dropped into the bubbling water to join their mother.

Clinging close to her side, they formed a compact little raft that quickly slipped downstream, carried along by the current until they overtook the madly paddling foursome.

With shrewd calculation, the mother had figured how she could use the current to her advantage in carrying out the rescue operation. She let it carry her and her disciplined little flock beyond the four paddlers so that she could intercept them before they reached the rapids.

Exhausted, they collided with her in her downstream course. The mother, spreading her wings ever so slightly, gathered them to her and guided all twelve ducklings to the safety of a quiet shallow pool near the opposite shore.

It was all over in a few breathless seconds. The frantic "beep-beep-beep" had stopped, and the only sound in the woods was the innocent burbling of the swift-running water.

Crows under Siege

THERE IS ALWAYS SOME APPREHENSION ABOUT NEW NEIGH-bors. For better or worse, one family can change the atmosphere very quickly. So we watched the beginning of construction with more than mere curiosity.

The new owners, showing the pride of possession, were on the scene every day quite early in the morning. We had seen them around the neighborhood before, usually following after the trucks on trash-collection days, and it was inevitable that they would discover on their rounds that Melody Lane has attractive home sites on wooded lots.

They chose an elm across the street from us and no doubt congratulated themselves on being the first crows on the block.

Over the years we have developed a certain respect for common crows with their uncommon intelligence, but we were not sure we would welcome them as close neighbors. To begin with, they are noisy. But to be fair, we have to admit that when a crow speaks, it pays to listen. He may be calling attention to a hawk or an owl.

Investigation of their clamor usually reveals that the crows are agitators, not innocent bystanders. In a favorite sport known as "mobbing," they gang up on other birds, in threes and fours and in larger flocks. I have seen them make life miserable for a great horned owl who wanted nothing but to be left alone while his mate sat on the nest. But once the crows discovered him, their cries summoned reinforcements, and the mob chased the owl from perch to perch, happy to devote their entire morning to the challenge.

I have watched crows harassing red-tailed hawks as well as mockingbirds, and on one occasion I watched a band of a dozen crows beat a red-tailed hawk to death. It took them half a day to do it, but they accomplished their mission by making repeated attacks on the hawk every time he flew up until finally, his wings tattered and his energy exhausted, he was forced down into a field and could never get airborne again. His attackers closed in for the kill, as if they had planned it that way.

To offset that picture of gang murder on an Idaho farm, I have a picture of common crows strutting around beneath the palms at Flamingo, in the Florida Everglades. In their strong beaks they were carrying rectangular white morsels that I identified as bars of guest soap, still in their paper wrappers bearing the label of the Flamingo Lodge.

Like magpies, crows will steal all kinds of useless articles that strike their fancy. But they also steal eggs from other birds' nests, not to mention young birds. So they have earned a bad reputation in the bird community as well as in the human community, and it is small wonder that the bluejays opened hostilities at the first signs of occupancy and did everything they could to discourage the new tenants.

From the kitchen window we watched their onslaughts. The attacking party of jays usually numbered six, all masters of harassment, and the crows had their claws full, fending off the enemy all the while they were building their home. But they persisted, even when the attacks came from all directions at once.

We had to admire their tenacity and became engrossed in the drama being played out against the skyline in full view of our window like a suspense-laden soap opera. We set up a spotting scope on a tripod and trained it on the developing nest so that we could watch daily progress. There were no leaves on the trees when the building project began in early March, so we had an unobstructed view of the nest in the top branches of the elm.

Returning home after a few days' absence, we found the new home completed and occupied. But it was under constant siege. The jays were still organized to rid themselves of their undesirable neighbors. All through the day, their vulgar screams disturbed the peace as they dive-bombed the nest.

The male crow, from his sentry post above the nest, counter-attacked, warding off from three to six jays at a time. He himself was the object of the attack much of the time, and we thought he would be worn down to a shadow before he became a parent—*if* he ever became a parent. Outnumbered and outflanked, his supply lines frequently cut off, he was having difficulty gathering food and delivering it to his brooding mate.

Then one night, when the couple must have been nearing exhaustion, a violent storm struck. We were wakened in the night by the howl of the wind and the cracking of tree limbs. At daybreak we marveled to find that the nest was still there in the elm, being lashed from side to side as heavy gusts bent the top branches.

Through the scope, we saw with some relief the low profile of the tenacious bird on the nest. Her mate was not in sight, nor were there any jays to terrorize her as the storm tossed her about, all that day and into the next.

When the winds diminished, the male appeared again

at his sentry post, prepared to do battle if necessary. It was not necessary. The jays did not return.

A leaf screen obscured the nest all too soon, so we were unable to watch the fledging of the young, and they were almost the size of their parents by the time we realized there were not two crows but five on our block.

To Save a Mockingbird

LAST NIGHT THE MOON WAS FULL AND BRIGHT. IT WAS THE kind of night that brings joy to the heart of the male mockingbird—and irritation to many a weary insomniac kept awake by his song. Listening to our own resident virtuoso, I could predict the series of telephone calls that would come in the morning.

Some callers, noting my connection with the Audubon Society, were ready to hold me personally accountable for what "my" birds had done to disrupt their sleep. Some called out of curiosity: What was the bird and why was he singing at night? Many appreciated the nocturnal serenade; others complained bitterly and wanted to know what they could do to prevent it, short of avicide.

Sandwiched between two such calls was an SOS from my neighbor across the street. A young bird was down in her window well screaming his head off, driving her mad. She thought it was injured. She feared it had been mauled by Cassidy, her cat.

I found Cassidy sitting on the grating over the window well, looking down with intense curiosity, but not a trace of guilt, at the squalling bird whose voice alone would have identified it as a mockingbird. It was quite young. It had virtually no tail, and its breast bore gray spots that would disappear as it matured—*if* it matured. It seemed to be all beak and gaping mouth. With head thrown back, it screamed lustily and constantly. Whatever damage it might have suffered, there was nothing wrong with its lungs.

The first step in the rescue was to banish Cassidy from the scene. The second step was to prepare a shoe box lined with soft tissue as a temporary home for the waif. Throughout these preparations we looked in vain for any sign of anxious parents, ready to take over the feeding.

Finding neither adult birds nor nearby nest, I removed the grating and reaching down, easily captured the youngster, put it into the box and took it home, fully aware of the responsibility I was undertaking. It would have to be fed every fifteen minutes, I knew, and after offering it grated tuna, which it ate ravenously, I called the Bird Rescue Team for further instructions.

The trained volunteer on call prescribed dog food, of all things—dry kibbles dissolved in hot water and administered at fifteen-minute intervals. On learning of the circumstances, and of Cassidy's acute interest in the scene, the volunteer warned: "If the cat actually got him, there isn't much hope. A pin-hole puncture from a cat's tooth or claw is very hard to find among all those feathers, so very often there's a small puncture to a vital organ and we don't even know it. The birds usually do all right for a couple of days, and then die very suddenly. But good luck—and call me back."

By midday my patient was still eating greedily but remaining fairly quiet between feedings, and I had adjusted to doing my chores in fifteen-minute spurts.

When I went out to drop a letter in the mailbox, I heard a mockingbird singing from a high wire, just across the street. That could be the parent, I thought, and hopefully I brought the shoebox out to the front yard with the lid open.

Clearly, the young bird recognized a familiar voice. It stretched its neck and turned its head in an alert pose, then gave a loud, answering cheep. Putting the box down under a tree, I stepped back to see what would happen.

Immediately the adult swooped down, hopped across the grass and looked into the box. He gave a harsh call, flew up into the tree, and was joined at once by a second mockingbird. Both began an agitated squawking, as unmusical as birds can be, while the youngster beneath them rivaled them both for volume and harshness of voice.

Did it recognize its parents? Was this a call for rescue from the wicked kidnapper?

I decided to liberate the captive from the box. It snapped at the hand that had fed it and screamed louder than ever, and when I set it down in the thick green grass, it went running pell-mell away from me, moving very quickly and with no sign of disability except for lifting one wing at an odd angle.

Now that the baby bird was out in the open, and I was a safe distance away, the parents might take over the feeding process and find more appropriate food for an infant than I had been providing. But they did no such thing. They hopped madly about in the tree, ignoring the youngster and squalling raucously at each other as if engaged in a bitter custody battle.

All the birds gathered around to witness the scene. House finches wheezed quizzically from the telephone wire. A cardinal dropped down in the grass beside the young mockingbird and examined it closely before returning to his own perch near a nest in the pin-oak. But the parent birds—if they were, indeed, the parents—continued their fussing at each other without giving any sign of taking over their responsibilities.

It was past feeding time. I recaptured the patient and offered it the standard dog-food ration, but it was so perturbed by the commotion all around that it refused to eat. Only when I took it indoors, beyond earshot of the quarreling adults, did it quiet down and take sustenance.

Once more I gave the adults a chance to do the right thing. Their behavior was completely baffling. As soon as they heard the young bird's cries, they resumed their quarreling.

In despair I gave up on them. Either these were not the rightful parents or they simply didn't know how to cope with a bird that had left the nest prematurely.

I called the Bird Rescue volunteer again. I was not competent to act *in loco parentis*, especially if the bird had internal injuries of which I was unaware. She agreed that it needed expert observation and care, as well as a flight cage, which she could provide.

We arranged a rendezvous at a shopping center, and at 3:00 P.M.—after administering one last feeding in the car—I turned my patient over to the expert, who observed that he was a spunky little fellow and just might make it.

Back home now, I am grappling with the empty-nest syndrome, rattling around aimlessly, looking at the clock every fifteen minutes, suppressing the impulse to call for hourly bulletins on my patient's progress. Cassidy strolls innocently across my lawn, and I wonder if he did leave an indiscernible pin-hole puncture in that small body. Or is he as blameless as he looks? Maybe the little bird simply fell from the nest and then down into the window well, where it captured Cassidy's attention with its screams.

But speculation is useless. I'll wait till tomorrow to call for a report. With luck and good care, this same little bird, a year from now, may be keeping someone awake with a joyful moonlight serenade.

Look What the Cat Dragged in!

A BIRD IN THE HAND IS NOT ALWAYS A SOURCE OF UN-adulterated pleasure. It can, in fact, be downright disconcerting, especially if it shows signs of having been mauled by a favorite cat.

Calls of distress from cat owners attest to the truth that one does not have to be anti-cat to be pro-bird.

"You have to live with them all," said one sad caller, "birds . . . cats . . . dogs."

One of her cats had brought in a bird that she could not identify. After leafing through her new Peterson guide, she concluded that it resembled more than anything else a paint-billed crake, listed among "Accidentals from the Tropics."

It was highly unlikely, she knew, that a bird could have wandered from Peru or the Galapagos to her back yard in Fairfax, Virginia. And anyway, it was not quite the same. Its legs were green istead of red, and its beak was red at the base, yellowish-green at the tip.

That was a puzzler. The most likely guess was a rail —something like a sora, for example, small enough for a cat to manage. But the field marks simply didn't fit.

As it turned out, identification was not a great problem. There was a *corpus delicti*. The bird, which was dead when Tiger brought it in, was now reposing in the freezer, carefully wrapped in plastic.

A local expert was quick to proclaim it a common gallinule (recently renamed common moorhen), a sizeable thirteen-inch bird.

The field marks were right, of course, but I could not imagine a cat bringing in so large a bird.

"You don't know Tiger," sighed the owner. "He's terrible. Our other three cats are very good. But we can't do a thing with Tiger. He even catches squirrels."

Her voice blended despair with a kind of grudging admiration.

There are protectionists among bird watchers who would have us destroy all feline predators. But most of us who enjoy birds and cats equally manage to strike some compromises.

"I try to keep Tiger in when there are young birds around," said the lady who had the moorhen in her freezer. "But it's hard. He howls and yells till he drives us crazy. He's just naturally an outdoors cat."

Outdoors cats, even if they are well fed, will inevitably catch birds from time to time. It's a natural game for a cat. And you have to admit that sometimes the victims ask for it. A taunting mockingbird or catbird is a prime target.

That's one way to rationalize it. Another is to console yourself with the thought that the bird was probably sick or injured already and would not have survived anyway. The moorhen, for example, showed no signs of mauling ("Tiger is well fed and rarely eats a bird he catches"), and the logical speculation was that the bird, migrating through Fairfax City, had struck a window and was already dead or dazed when Tiger found it.

I am sympathetic to that theory. In the days when we kept outdoor cats, I would sometimes observe a sluggish, sickly bird among the juncos in the back yard, and

I was able to predict with some assurance that the bird would show up in the cat's mouth later in the day.

One day a large flock of cedar waxwings stopped off to feed in our crabtree, and when they took off they left behind one straggler who appeared to be unwell. For the whole afternoon he sat shivering on the lowest branch of the tree. Next morning his inert body was brought to me as a present by our top cat. One is expected to show appreciation for these unwelcome gifts.

Cats often prove to be great connoisseurs of birds, disdaining the common, abundant species. Impartial as we may try to be, it is undeniably harder to grieve over a lost house sparrow or starling than, say, a magnolia warbler or a thrush. Friends sadly admit that their cats never bring in anything but cardinals and robins.

We once had a cat that specialized in Carolina wrens. That was in the days before the species suffered a rapid population decline, but even so, a Carolina wren is a very special little bird. We had to admit that Remus had good taste.

Fortunately, he also had a soft mouth and the best of intentions. He brought them alive, often kicking and squalling in his mouth, and presented them with obvious pride. Often I heard the bird's screams before Remus emerged through the cat-port into the kitchen, and I was ready to cope with the situation.

It happened often enough that I developed a fail-proof life-saving technique. It took about five seconds.

The first step was to startle the poor cat with a sharp, unexpected "Kitty, no!" Then, when he stopped short, I startled him further with a smart tap on the nose. At this, his jaw dropped open and the wren fell into my waiting hand. In six steps I was across the kitchen to the window, and the bird was set free.

Then it was time to give the bewildered cat the praise he had been expecting.

I don't know what I would have done if he had brought me a gallinule.

Cardinals and Roses

"IT'S NOT WORTH BRAIN SPACE," MY MOTHER WOULD SAY, and of course it isn't. But memory is undiscriminating and intractable, so I am stuck with it. Every spring, when the first robins appear in the back yard, it comes back to haunt me—that silly, romantic song all about robins and roses around the honeymoon cottage, where, presumably, the young couple will live happily ever after.

Why don't I just forget it? I didn't even like it when I was young and romantic. Not that I was averse to romance. It was the association of robins and roses that bothered me. They just didn't go together.

We all make our own associations, based on experience, and I'd much rather give brain space to my childhood memories of robins and maple blossoms—although in those days I thought they were maple *buds* that shattered over the new-green grass and made a red path in the bare patch under the swing.

With little effort of imagination, I can recall the raw

chill of an early spring rain, the smell of wet earth and drowned earthworms, the sight of fat worms wriggling in tiny rainpools under the swing, and opportunistic robins running along over the fallen red blossoms, looking for an easy meal.

Robins and maple blossoms—a little unwieldy for the songwriter. How about robins and snowdrops? That's a good combination. Or robins and tulips. But not robins and roses. By the time the roses were in bloom, robins, busy with domestic chores, were not much in evidence.

I can link other birds with roses, as long as I don't have the songwriter's problems of rhyme and meter. I think of chickadees, for example, for I have watched them patiently stripping aphids off the thorny rose canes.

Then there were the mockingbirds that always declared our own rose garden off limits to us during the nesting season and dive-bombed us mercilessly if we lingered around it long enough to cut a blossom or two. The roses were much too close to the mockingbird's nest in the nearby hemlock hedge.

But most of all, I think of cardinals and roses, because of one pair of cardinals that nested in the crimson rambler just outside the back door.

I worried about them when they started building so close to the house, and in such an accessible spot, only five or six feet from the ground. But after all, I reflected, birds are at least as alert to predators as I am, and they must have put their faith in the rambler's heavy thorns to protect them from cats, their most likely enemy.

The site seemed to be the choice of the lady cardinal, who must have seen the advantage of using the crossbar of the trellis for a foundation, and as chief architect she placed the structure so that it was well screened by dense foliage. I might have overlooked it myself if I had not seen the birds building it.

From the kitchen window I could watch the progress of the project as the rambler buds burst into blossoms. The female did most of the work while the male cheered her on. Occasionally he brought an offering—a twig or a scrap of dried weed-stalk—that she would examine critically and sometimes reject. When it came to the finishing touches—fine little fibers and wispy tendrils of dry grass—she did it all herself.

It took nearly a week of painstaking labor, and just when it appeared to be completed, she abandoned the nest. Did it fall short of her standards? Or had she become aware of some safety hazard? I did not know. All I knew was that the cardinal couple disappeared, and after two or three days I became resigned to the loss.

Then suddenly one morning I heard the male's cheeriest song ringing out. From the kitchen window, I saw the female sitting contentedly on the nest, all framed with crimson roses. It was all right, after all.

Our of respect for her privacy and peace of mind, we stopped using the back door, which opened only a few feet from the nest, but she seemed undisturbed by our comings and goings inside the kitchen and our discreet peeks out the window.

The solicitous male brought food to her and once took her place on the nest while she went out for her own. On one occasion when she left the nest briefly, I climbed up on the kitchen counter so that I could look down into the nest. The view was partially obstructed by overhanging roses, but I did see two eggs, both a dull gray-green with splotches of brown.

We checked off the days on the calendar, knowing that we could expect a twelve-day incubation period. Unfortunately, we had to be away for a weekend, so we missed the main event. When we came back, we found the parents settled into an efficient feeding pattern.

To our suprise, they had four mouths to feed.

They were noisy mouths, too, always open, always screaming. The young birds' cries became our background music day after day, replacing the music of the father, who was now too busy to sing. Through the kitchen window, now open to the warm spring air, I

listened to the young family's insistent demands while
I prepared breakfast for my own family.

On the fifth morning the noise was missing. An eerie
silence once again fell over the back yard, just as it had
when the cardinal couple had mysteriously disappeared,
leaving the unoccupied nest.

Once again the nest was unoccupied.

But it was too soon, I thought in a sudden panic. The
birds were surely too young to fly.

I hurried to the reference shelf and looked up "Cardinals" once again. I was right. "The young remain in
the nest for nine or ten days."

Cardinal

But they were gone. Something had happened in the night, something the dazed mother didn't understand. For when I returned to the kitchen, she was standing on the edge of the nest with an offering of food, and no mouths were there to claim it.

For two days she continued to make regular trips to the empty nest, carrying food. Her devoted mate was nowhere to be seen.

Then, on the third day, I heard his cheering, persuasive notes on the other side of the hemlock hedge. She heard, too, and abandoned the lost cause. It was time to try again.

The Odyssey of a Baby Wood Duck

It is a rare thing to have the canal towpath all to yourself on a fine May day, but the migration was behind schedule and there were neither birds nor birders along the C&O Canal as I set out for a lone walk from Violet's Lock to Pennyfield.

Encumbered by a temporary "walking cast," I stumped along the historic path, hardened long ago by mule teams towing barges on the canal that George Washington had envisioned as a vital trade link between the capital and the Ohio River. Now the path is traveled by hikers and bikers, campers and birders, thousands of them, attracted by its rare scenic beauty, with broad vistas of the Potomac River on one side and the canal on the other.

"Justice Douglas's Canal," we call it, for it was the efforts of a busy Supreme Court Justice that saved all this from being transformed into a rushing highway paralleling the river. I have often regretted not having joined the throng of supporters that accompanied William O. Douglas on his historic 185-mile hike the length of the towpath, from Cumberland to Georgetown, to dramatize the importance of maintaining this as a great natural resource. His vision prevailed over that of the highway builders, for which I am constantly grateful, for some of the most beautiful stretches of the towpath are only minutes away from our door and offer prime birding, especially in migration, when waves of warblers come through.

The mile and a half from Violet's Lock to Pennyfield, with its rugged cliffs and serene waters, is especially popular and usually populous. On weekends it can be uncomfortably crowded at times; even on weekdays, it is rarely deserted. But I walked for fifteen minutes without encountering another soul.

I was within sight of Blockhouse Point before I saw or heard a single sign of birdlife. And then, far ahead of me, I saw a small wake in the water, too small a wake to be created by a duck. Possibly a pied-billed grebe, I thought.

Increasing my pace for a closer look, I found that it was a duck, after all—a very small, downy duckling, newly hatched, apparently lost from his flock. He seemed to know exactly where he was going, for he paddled determinedly toward Pennyfield, emitting small "cheeps" at regular intervals.

Since we were traveling in the same direction, I slowed down to keep pace with him and watched for the moment of a reunion that never came.

Together we rounded Blockhouse Point, he in midstream, I on the upper level of the towpath looking down at him. By that time I knew, from his light eyemark and his red-tipped bill, that my little traveling companion was a young wood duck, probably just out of his nest.

He proceeded purposefully for a few yards beyond Blockhouse Point, and then some unseen force shattered his confidence. The moment of truth had come: He was lost, and he knew it.

Faltering in indecision, he went completely out of control, screaming frantically and swimming around and around in tight circles.

His cries brought immediate attention—not from an adult wood duck, but from the whole bird community that had been silent and invisible until then. Now suddenly they were all there to investigate the distressed cries. Bluejays, as usual, were in the lead, followed by cardinals, titmice, and chickadees buzzing excitedly. Tree swallows materialized from nowhere. A phoebe appeared on an overhanging branch. A catbird squalled, and even a little yellowthroat joined the onlookers.

They were no help to the little waif in the water. Fluttering and dive-bombing over him, they drowned out his screams with their own.

I watched helplessly from the bank. I was in no position to play the rescuer role. Even if the water were shallow—and I was not at all sure it was—I couldn't plunge in with that heavy cast on my left leg. Yet I couldn't simply walk away and let the inevitable happen.

In desperation, I began to make soft noises: "Sh-sh-sh-sh!" imitating the rhythm of the duckling's cries. Amazingly, it captured his attention as well as that of his hecklers, who began to disperse as soon as the little duck calmed down.

Left to ourselves, we carried on a ship-to-shore communication of sorts:

"Cheep-cheep-cheep-cheep!"

"Sh-sh-sh-sh!"

When I turned back toward Violet's Lock, he turned and followed me. That one constant sound guided him.

I don't know what I had in mind, except the hope that somewhere along the way we would find a wood duck family, or a wood duck nest in a tree cavity near the water. If I found no distraught mother searching for him, maybe I could find some human help back at Violet's Lock.

Maintaining constant voice contact, we moved slowly toward the goal, a mile away. It was like walking with a toddler, but the toddler would not take my hand. He stayed out in mid-canal all the while, occasionally snapping at something on the water's surface. It encouraged me to think he was getting sustenance for the long journey, but I was fearful that the ordeal would be too much for so young a swimmer.

There were perils along the way: a snake basking on a sun-warmed log; a turtle surfacing dangerously close to a mouthful of duckling. Some floating debris threw the little fellow into a state of confusion, and he did an about-face and began swimming back toward Blockhouse Point.

It took all my powers of persuasion to get him to turn and follow me.

Another time he was startled by a pair of whooping bicyclists who whizzed past me without looking to right or left. But after spinning in a circle for a time, he righted his course and we continued on our way.

We had covered more than half the distance when I heard, with a swell of hope, a familiar "Whoo-eek, Whoo-eek!" A pair of wood ducks flew directly over us on their way to the river. They paid no attention to us. If they heard the duckling's cries, it was no concern of theirs.

As they disappeared beyond the trees I turned my thoughts to plotting a human rescue. I would need help. And, luckily, help was in sight at Violet's Lock, where a young man was launching a kayak. I hailed him and enlisted his willing aid.

Carefully, he maneuvered the kayak past the little duck and then, edging along behind him, forced him in toward the bank where I was standing. Trapped between bank and kayak, the duckling did the natural thing: He took a dive into the shallow water.

The young man in the kayak moved quickly. Plunging his arm down into the water, he captured a handful of vegetation with a screaming little duck in the midst of it. He gazed at it in wonder. He had never held a wood duck before.

Neither had I. When he delivered it to me, the sharp claws, designed for climbing trees, dug into my palms. The red-tipped bill clamped down on my finger. And then he hissed at me. After all we had been through together.

Twenty minutes later he was swimming happily in my blue bathtub while I made telephone calls to the Bird Rescue volunteers who are on call to give expert advice.

They were helpful but not overly encouraging. They had seen it happen many times. Wood duck mothers apparently can't count. They are unlikely to notice if one of a brood of a dozen or so is slow leaving the nest or lags behind in the water when they go for their first swim. Their lost babies are often found along the canal in the spring, but even with the best of care, they seldom survive.

Despite these voices of experience, I remained optimistic, ready to reorganize my life around the spunky little fellow who had survived the long march with me.

He swam energetically, climbed the shower curtain, ate the prescribed offerings at fifteen-minute intervals, and hissed every time I approached. With that kind of spirit, he would surely make it.

He was probably only a day old when I found him, and he died a day later, leaving me to contemplate on the many lives that had been touched by his brief existence, and on the wisdom of the mother wood duck who cannot count her ducklings but nevertheless holds secrets of survival that we may never know.

Crash Landing

IT WAS THE WORST KIND OF WEATHER, THE KIND THAT spells disaster.

The storm that hit the Washington area at mid-afternoon reached its peak in time for the evening rush hour. Snow turning to freezing rain and sleet iced the highways and created traffic havoc throughout the metropolitan area. Visibility was low; tempers and apprehension ran high.

As meteorologists droned on about the "weather system" that was causing this chaos, commuters crawling across the Potomac bridges were haunted by memories of the Air Florida flight that had crashed immediately after takeoff from National Airport in 1982, plunging its passengers into the icy waters of the Potomac.

All the conditions were there for another such disaster. The law of averages seemed to decree it as the storm continued through the night. Gusts of wind rattled sleet against the windows of restless sleepers. At dawn, anxieties were put to rest when the morning news came on with no report of anything worse than fender-benders.

No one knew, yet, that there had been a dozen crash landings in the metropolitan area that night, and that stranded victims were scattered about on highways and suburban parking lots.

I had no idea of the magnitude of the disaster when I received my first telephone call of the day. Like so many calls that come to me, it was a request for help in identifying a strange bird, which usually turns out to be a house finch or some kind of sparrow.

But this was a large bird, "as heavy as a Thanksgiving turkey," said the woman, who thought that it was some kind of duck because it had webbed feet. But the bill was straight, she said, not flat like a duck's bill. She described the black head, the dark back with white speckling on the wings, the pure white breast—pure white except for the blood that stained it.

Unfortunately, the bird was dead.

"It's the most beautiful thing I ever saw," she said sadly. "I picked it up on the parking lot at my supermarket last night around nine o'clock. I have no idea what it is or what it would be doing there."

I knew what it was. She had given a good description of a common loon—uncommon in these parts at any time, and most uncommon on dry land. We sometimes see them flying over in migration, singly or in groups of two or three, and during the winter months we see them occasionally on the Potomac or on inland lakes and ponds. But on land, never.

I could only speculate that this migrating loon, forced down by the severe storm, had spotted the lighted parking lot and, mistaking its wet surface for a body of water, had come down for a surprise crash landing. It may have struck something—a wire, a pole, a car—as it landed; or it may have survived the crash, only to be struck by a car after landing. We would never know the story.

But before the day was over, we knew that this was not the only loon that had crashed in the night. It was the only loon that had not survived. The others—eleven of them, as the reports came in from scattered points around the county—were in grave trouble and waiting to be rescued. Unlike the victims of the Air Florida crash, who had to be saved from the icy water, these victims had to be returned to the water, no matter how icy, in order to survive.

The loons' lives were endangered not only by the foul weather on their migration route, but also by their own anatomical shortcomings, which render them virtually helpless on land, unable to take off again once they are grounded.

Call it faulty design or a rare mistake of nature. It is, actually, a compromise of nature. The loon is designed for a watery habitat. He is a superb diver (in Britain he is known, appropriately, as the Great Northern Diver) and a powerful underwater swimmer. His feet, set far back on his body, serve as strong propellers. His wings, slender in proportion to his body, give him the stream-lining that makes for efficient swimming and flight. But these same features handicap him for the takeoff. Even on water, he has to struggle to become airborne, pad-dling furiously for a hundred yards or so before his wings can lift him up. On land, this is impossible. Poorly balanced on his rear-mounted legs, he can scarcely walk, much less get the running start he would need to take to the air.

Only human intervention could save the grounded loons. Rescuers from the U.S. Fish and Wildlife Service responded to the emergency, picking up the helpless birds where they had crashed—on highways and park-ing lots, at shopping malls and even in a suburban back yard.

Miraculously, their injuries were minor, considering the circumstances of their landing on unyielding sur-faces. Most of the damage was to their landing gear.

Bruised and bleeding feet were treated by experts at the Bird Rehabilitation Center, where all the victims were pronounced fit for release.

For eleven loons there was a happy ending when they were restored to their natural habitat. Escaping the horrors of *terra firma*, they plunged happily into the cold waters of Chesapeake Bay and did what they were designed to do best. They dove out of sight of their rescuers.

Loon

Wrens in Jeopardy

It is far from being a silent spring, but something is missing in the morning medley of bird song. The voice of the Carolina wren has not been heard on Melody Lane this year. Its absence is noticeable because this is a voice we are accustomed to hearing in all seasons.

The Carolina wren is a year-round resident, and one of the few species of birds that sing 365 days a year, so his voice has become a part of the background sound that assures us that all's well.

But all is not well this spring. The voice that is missing from Melody Lane is missing, too, from Hughes Hollow, and Seneca, and all along the towpath where the male's familiar "teakettle song" and the female's answering "churrr" had become so common they were almost ignored by sophisticated birders listening for seldom-heard voices.

Now the alarming reports come in after every field trip: "Not a single Carolina wren." Or, occasionally, an exclamation: "Heard *two Carolina wrens!*"—as if reporting a rarity.

In our own walks along the C&O Canal we have heard the cheery song only four times this year, and each time was an occasion for rejoicing. The only Carolina wren we have actually seen since Christmastime was a dead one found in early March, lying in a stubblefield near Sycamore Landing, one of the many victims of winter-kill.

Unfortunately, Carolina wrens are not constituted to withstand harsh winters and are in peril where they extend their range to its northernmost limits. Being non-migratory, they have no impulse to head south when temperatures drop below normal and their food supplies are placed in deep-freeze. They feed on or near the ground on a diet of insects, insect eggs, and spiders, which were difficult to find during the past winter when snow and ice-glaze persisted for a period of weeks. Their beaks are not adapted to seed eating, so they cannot make substitutions as other species do in times of stress. Their habits and limitations make them vulnerable to extremes of weather in their northern outposts.

How many Carolina wrens were lost in this record-breaking winter remains to be determined from May bird censuses and banding reports. But the numbers must be great, for a succession of unusually mild winters had produced a population explosion. In our own Christmas Count sector, we had seen the totals climb from 171 to 465 and up to a record high of 819.

It was on that count that I saw my last Carolina wren and marked him on my tally sheet as No. 16 for the day, with no thought that this might become a memorable sighting. I heard his call from a thicket—not the "teakettle song," but the two-syllable song, equally loud and clear, that I translate as "Gertie, Gertie, Gertie!"

His mate, who seems to answer to that name, responded from across the canal, whereupon he flew out in the open, perched on a low branch, and rendered another selection from his varied repertoire. This time it was a different three-note call, with a heavy accent on the second note, and I interpreted it as "Come *see* me, come *see* me, come *see* me!'' The female did not respond to the invitation, so I did not see her. But I took time to enjoy the picture of the small chestnut-backed bird on the limb, his head thrown back, his buffy throat vibrating as he threw his whole heart and body into a song that rivaled that of the cardinal for volume and clarity.

I had seen the picture often enough in my own back yard where Carolina wrens, browsing around the porch foundations for spiders or sampling our offerings of suet, would interrupt their feeding with bursts of exuberant song. But I have a precise memory of that wren at

Carolina Wren

Pennyfield last December because it happened to be quite near the site of a nest I had observed two years earlier. An unusually daring pair of wrens had selected a tree cavity in full view of the towpath, no more than five feet from the ground. Hundreds of bikers and hikers and equestrians passed by within a few feet of the nest, while the unobtrusive little wrens came and went, feeding their young, whose hungry cries were quite audible to ears attuned to bird voices.

Those four little birds with their wide-open mouths were part of the baby boom that brought the Christmas Count that year to a total of 762.

It will take many years and a series of mild winters to build back up to that level. Meanwhile, we will listen for the song of the Carolina wren as we listen for a rare bird, and its song will be a reminder of the fragility of life and the hazards of the frontier.

An Owl, a Cardinal, and a Sandpiper

POE HAD HIS RAVEN, BUT I HAVE THREE BIRDS THAT HAUNT me: a cardinal, a solitary sandpiper, and a great horned owl.

Four birds, actually, because there were two of the owls. It looked at first like only one, lying by the roadside. But when we stopped to examine the heap of feathers, we found them huddled close together, an adult and a youngster, possibly out on his first training flight, which also turned out to be his last. The two limp bodies, still warm, bore no mark of the recent violence.

There was no human sound to break the stillness that surrounded us as we stood looking down at the picture of parent and offspring. It was as if we had the whole world to ourselves. We had not seen a single car on the road since setting out at dawn. But somewhere ahead on that gray stretch of highway was the car that had struck them.

I plucked a perfect cream-and-buff feather from each of them. Already, two silent vultures were circling impatiently overhead.

That was in Arizona. Miles away, in Maryland, and years away in time, we walked into a wildlife refuge where again we had the world to ourselves. We had walked for more than two hours without encountering another human. The only signs of civilization were the occasional planes passing overhead and, at intervals along the way, the metal signs marking the boundary of the refuge, rusted with age and pockmarked with bullet holes.

Following a bend in the trail at the edge of the woods, we came upon one of those lovely, peaceful scenes that capture the essence of what we are seeking when we go afield. In a shallow rainpool that reflected the brilliance of the April sky, a lone shorebird was feeding tranquilly as if he, too, had the world to himself.

Not wanting to intrude, we stopped at a safe distance. We were still close enough to see the tiny ripples he stirred as he picked his way delicately along the fringe of the pool. By the gentle bobbing of his head and the white ring around his bright, alert eye, we knew without even raising our binoculars that he was a solitary sandpiper. The name had never seemed more appropriate. He was the picture of solitude, unaware even of our presence.

Taking careful steps backwards, we withdrew around the bend in the trail and made a wide circle around to avoid disturbing him.

An hour later we returned the same way and approached the spot cautiously, hoping for one more glimpse of our lone sandpiper, our bird of the day.

He was still there. His body was stretched out at the edge of the rainpool, his fragile, graceful legs submerged in the shallow water, his bloody head lying in the soft mud.

With a sickening sense of an evil presence that had violated his solitude, and ours, we went on our way. Minutes later we encountered the only people we had seen all day: two teenage boys, both with rifles. They were target shooting, they said, and they had none of the aura of evil. But we knew that a boy with a gun becomes a different boy. Temptations and challenges shout at him. Rusted old "No Hunting" signs are fair enough game, but the only real way to prove your skill is with a moving target.

We could produce no evidence, make no charges, but they knew that we knew what their target had been.

We had not even heard the shot that had blasted the peace of that perfect day, but its echo has been with me through the years. I have never looked at a solitary sandpiper since without seeing *the* solitary sandpiper, in all his innocence and perfection.

Cardinals I see every day of the year, but there was a special cardinal, long ago in a wooded area in the Virginia countryside where we were looking for a home.

On that fresh spring day with the sunlight filtering through the new leaves on the hillside and highlighting the waves on the Potomac River down below, any house would have been attractive. The real estate agent saw that we were enchanted by the setting, and she extolled the virtues of the builder, who had carefully preserved the fine old trees, and the architect, who had designed the house to afford inspiring views on every side.

Pointing to the generous expanse of windows across the front, she proclaimed, "This is a house that invites the outdoors in."

At that moment a male cardinal appeared, as if on cue, to punctuate her well-rehearsed line. He flew out of the light-and-shadow of a tulip poplar into a shaft of sunlight directly in front of us, his scarlet plumage so intense a hue that all of us caught a quick breath of wonder. Someone, maybe all three of us, said, "Look at—"

The sentence ended in a horrifying thud as the cardinal struck the polished glass that was designed to invite the outdoors in.

A cardinal, a solitary sandpiper, and two great horned owls: three dissimilar species, widely separated in the time and space of my experience, forever linked together in my consciousness. They haunt me, not with cries of "Nevermore," nor with the well-worn message of life's brevity, but with the vision of myself and my kind as intruders and destroyers. We observe, we appreciate, we protect, but even in our most innocent pursuits, we inadvertently destroy.

I can deplore reckless driving and the wanton use of firearms. I can indulge in blameless grief for the lost owls and the sandpiper. But there is still the cardinal to haunt me with the reminder that they who build glass houses in the quiet woods also destroy.

PART SIX

The Christmas Count

Why Do We Do It?

I HUM TO MYSELF AS I SET OUT THE GEAR FOR YET ANOTHER Christmas Bird Count, knowing that the irrevocably appointed day may bring rain, sleet, snow, wind, or freezing temperatures. We have had all those. We have had balmy days, too, when the comfort index was high and the bird count was low.

Rain is the worst, as we all know. Birds are under cover, and the meager results at the end of the day hardly justify the hours of slithering in mud, keeping tally on soggy checklists, and struggling to keep glasses and binoculars dry. Think positive. Think of clear skies and good visibility.

Blue skies . . . nothing but blue skies . . . I change my tune—and lay out armor against the worst that can come: down jackets, ski masks, windbreakers, wetsuits, boots, gloves, extra socks. Nothing short of a blizzard ever stops a Christmas Bird Count.

Tradition is powerful. This tradition goes back to Christmas Day in 1900, when twenty-seven birders established an alternative to the Christmas Day hunt, popular among sportsmen who, as Dr. Frank Chapman said, took to the fields and woods "on the cheerful mission of killing practically everything in fur or feathers that crossed their path—if they could." Dr. Chapman and his companions went out with the goal of counting every bird in their given territories and publishing the results, thereby providing an example in conservation as well as a census of winter bird populations.

The tradition caught on quickly among bird clubs, and what began as a casual afternoon stroll became an all-out, do-or-die, dawn-to-dark effort carried on by participants in every state of the Union and in Canada as well. The National Audubon Society became the sponsor of the annual event, which extended over a two-week period at Christmastime, laying down the ground rules and publishing the results.

My husband, Ted, and I got caught up in the tradition in 1969, our first year of birding. We know what to expect when the December date rolls around.

No matter what the weather, I know that the day will begin the same as it always has. In silence. After the apologetic beep of the alarm in the middle of the night, we go through the familiar ritual. Having birded together for sixteen years, we have learned when to hold our tongues. Breakfast is a time to turn off the sound.

It's pure theater: the casting, the costumes, the rehearsals. The show will go on. One more performance. The props are all ready. In silence, we load them into the car: flashlight, lunch, thermos, scope, clipboard, checklists . . . .

The curtain goes up. Ted always has the first line.

"Do we have everything?"

Yes, we have everything—everything but the answer to the inevitable question that comes up every year, raised mainly by reporters assigned to do a humor piece on the Christmas Bird Count: Why do we do it, year after year?

Searching for answers that would make sense to a

non-birder, I reflect on Christmas Counts past. I recall most vividly a dull, overcast day when the lighting was exceptionally poor for bird identification. Then, in the late afternoon, the sky cleared and the lowering sun washed the landscape in gold. Four of us, trudging the trail upriver to see what ducks might have come in for the night, reached the overlook point in time to see the sun drop behind the trees on the Virginia side. The river in front of us was smooth and serene, reflecting the cool turquoise of the winter sky, with accents of sunset gold. There was no ripple on the water, no wake to betray the presence of a raft of ducks.

No one minded. Relaxed and peaceful, we surveyed the scene, reluctant to leave, although we had been out before dawn to listen for owls. Then, as the sky darkened to a deep blue, at last the ducks began to appear. Flock after flock splashed down, disturbing the quiet water: buffleheads, scaup, goldeneyes, mallards, and mergansers—all coming in to rest. It was the grand finale signaling the final curtain.

That scene might help to explain the "why," but it has no place in a humor piece. Reporters, let's face it, find us amusing—and the Christmas Count gives them a prime opportunity to be witty. *'Tis the season to be jolly* . . . . Let them have their fun. We can afford to stand back, after the day's count, and see ourselves as others see us.

On the first day of Christmas . . . .

The words ring a bell in my memory and send me searching through my Christmas Bird Count file for a special clipping. It is Paul Sampson's account of the annual ritual, written for the National Geographic News Service in 1971:

> On the first day of Christmas, dedicated bird watchers rise at dawn to seek—not a partridge in a pear tree, but perhaps a red-eyed vireo. On the first day of the New Year, red-eyed bird watchers rouse themselves

Mallard Ducks

from dreams to see, perchance, the blue-faced booby.

The birders, 15,000 strong [who would believe that that number would swell to more than 38,000 by 1985], get up with the lark and 700 other species to take part in the National Audubon Society's Christmas Bird Count throughout the United States and Canada. The census indicates bird population trends and migration patterns. But the counters enjoy it primarily as a sport—a mammoth tournament of bird spotting. . . .

Counters endure all manner of hardships. Members of the birding team at Cape Kennedy, Florida, strap aluminum snake guards on their legs and wade through mosquito-infested swamps to break their record for the most species seen in one day. A Connecticut birder picks his way across a slippery log anchored three inches below the surface of a frigid stream. He is rewarded with the sight of a pine grosbeak—and wet feet. In Aklavik, deep in the Canadian north, two bird watchers spend five hours in 10-below-zero weather and see just two species—the willow ptarmigan and the common raven. Nevermore, they say.

Of course they don't really say, "Nevermore." That's what Sampson, an avowed non-birder, thought they should have said. But he had the grace to pay tribute to the hardy types we all admire: "Ornithologists have fallen from cliffs and trees," he wrote. "They have broken arms, legs, and ribs. They have been chased by tribesmen, robbed by bandits, charged by bulls. A leading British bird photographer lost an eye to a tawny owl he was documenting."

But Sampson is only human. He had to end it all with a funny story, because birders are very funny people. So he told the tale of Roger Tory Peterson himself, who was teamed up with four colleagues:

They were sitting in a car parked on a roadside at 3:00 A.M. A flashlight suddenly blazed upon the five, and a state trooper growled, "What do you guys think you're doing?" Silence. Then Mr. Peterson explained, "We're listening for whip-poor-wills." The men were promptly hustled off and held for several hours until they could tell it to a justice of the peace. He laughed and let them go."

It's the kind of story we tell among ourselves in the warmth of the tally rally at the end of the day's trials, when we gather to share our results. Outsiders like Paul Sampson would find only added amusement in the logical, all-important follow-up question: "Did anyone get the whip-poor-wills?"

Why do we do it?

Because we can't disappoint our public. We don't care if it rains or freezes. The show must go on. The costumes are ready—not shining armor, but the comic garb of clowns. Pagliacci is ready.

Vesti la giubba . . . .

An Indoor Christmas Bird Count

WHILE HARDY BIRDERS EVERYWHERE PREPARE TO GO AFIELD, in fair weather or foul, for the annual Christmas Bird Count, less venturesome souls have a splendid opportunity to conduct their own counts indoors by a cozy fire. Holiday greeting cards provide a veritable bird bonanza.

My own tally so far is twenty-one species and 745 individuals—not bad for an area confined to two Venetian blinds.

The rarest species to date is the kiwi, sent by an old friend who disappeared Down Under some years ago.

Canada geese, always pictured in flocks, win the numbers game, with cardinals a close second. (How could you face Christmas without cardinals in the snow?)

I have no loons or grebes in my collection, but one pair of mute swans floats on an ice-blue lake, and ducks are abundant this year.

Yesterday I was convinced that the mallard is the only duck known to greeting-card artists, but today a pair of green-winged teal appeared to prove me wrong. (For a midwinter scene, I would have chosen buffleheads, riding the Potomac rapids.)

Bobwhites are more numerous on paper this year than they have been in the field, and one pair of pheasants —or, rather, two cock pheasants in all their splendor, probably destined for a hunter's Christmas dinner— have just arrived.

Hawks and vultures are totally absent (I suppose a turkey vulture would be unseemly on Christmas Day), as are coots and gallinules. I miss the shorebirds, too. Surely there ought to be a few purple sandpipers, at least.

Gulls were never prominent on the Christmas scene until Jonathan Livingston Seagull made his debut a few years ago, but by now they are again on the decline. This year I found only one, with field marks that defy identification.

No terns. But what do you expect?

You can expect the dove of peace—right after the cardinal, numerically, even though it always appears solo, never in flocks.

Of course the dove of peace is not to be confused with our mourning dove. Lovely to look at, with his soft, subtle coloring, he sits on the feeder for hours, like a dog in the manger, too full to swallow another bite, too lazy to move on, keeping all the other birds away. He has a nasty disposition and can be intimidated only by bluejays (sometimes) and the red-bellied woodpecker, who occasionally sails in to the feeder emitting a menacing gurgle that would frighten any incumbent away.

Woodpeckers are not popular on Christmas cards. Only one—a little downy woodpecker—appears on this year's tally. He appears on the card that wins first prize for Greatest Number of Species per Tree, where I found an unlikely assembly of ten species adorning what appears to be a bare-branched willow. Each bird is resplendent in finest spring plumage against the snowy background: bluejays, chickadees, titmice, nuthatches (no brown creepers, however), a robin, two kinglets, cedar waxwings, the obligatory cardinal, a couple of pine siskins, white-throated sparrows, and juncos—not to mention both purple finches and goldfinches, dressed just as they were in the middle of May.

What lured this grand assortment to one fragile, seed-less tree is anyone's guess. Perhaps it gives them the view of a window beyond which a slothful provider of birdseed is sleeping late on Christmas morning.

Owls are abundant this year, as always. But the Christmas card count gives a distorted picture of bird populations generally. For example, I never see a house sparrow on a holiday greeting—or a starling, or a crow, or any of the birds of dark plumage. I miss them.

But most of all, I miss the mockingbird, the bird for all seasons, which serenades me on moonlit spring nights with songs of pure rapture and which wakes me on Christmas morning with harsh, unmusical demands for raisins—on the double.

Remembering his springtime arias, I forgive him his winter ill temper and watch him retreat in raisin-stuffed contentment to his favorite holly tree.

That's what I choose for my Christmas greeting—a lone mockingbird, *Mimus polyglottis*, singing from the topmost branch of a holly. Speaking in many tongues, he could carry the message of joy to the world in any language you choose: *Feliz Navidad!* . . . *Glad Jul!* . . . *Joyeux Noël!* . . . Merry Christmas!

The Unheard Song of a Sparrow

YESTERDAY'S STORM BROUGHT A WAVE OF WHITE-THROATED sparrows to our back yard this morning, and with them the reminder that it's time to gear up for another Christmas Count. We have been through it many times, my husband and I, and we are conditioned to accept any kind of weather: snowy, rainy, windy, balmy. But through all these variables, one thing remains the same: The day begins with white-throated sparrows.

Their "zeet, zeet" is the first sound I hear when I step from the car in the pre-dawn darkness. As we walk down the towpath, I hear them on all sides, calling from every bush and thicket. In my head I count the "zeets," which later become a row of black marks marching across the white page of my tally sheet. At the end of the day Ted will examine it and register amazement.

"That many white-throats?"

Not that he questions my integrity as the tally-keeper for the team. It's just that he doesn't hear them. He has a clear idea of how many white-throats he has seen, but this is always a mere fraction of the number I have heard.

Like many men his age, he is a victim of presbycussis, which in his offhand manner he translates as "old ears." It is a minor handicap, affecting men more than women, and at an earlier age. Technology has not yet provided a satisfactory correction for it.

To the average person it presents no real problem. But it is a special handicap for serious birders, depriving them of the ability to hear notes in the higher frequency range: those of kinglets, cedar waxwings, brown creepers, most of the warblers, and many of the sparrows.

Thus deprived, birders make their own adjustments. It is not surprising that they turn their attention to raptors and woodpeckers, shorebirds and waterfowl—birds they can enjoy without the audio cue. Ted made this adjustment without complaint.

So as we set out on our Christmas Count, the division of responsibility is predetermined: He carries the scope; I carry the clipboard. Long before daybreak, I am busy keeping score of that unseen world, sorting out all the miscellaneous chips and cheeps, zips and zeets, that are not within my companion's range.

It is not a great loss, he assures me, to miss the call of an unseen bird. But it is something of a shock to watch a bird throw back its head to sing and hear no note come from its vibrating throat. And it is sad to miss the marvelously lyrical song of the white-throated sparrow.

It became a mutual loss when we realized that this was a treasured experience we could no longer share.

By that time, he was missing warbler songs in the spring, but none of these were as important as those of the white-throated sparrow, who holds a special place in our hierarchy of birds. For this is one we discovered all by ourselves and identified by book. What a prideful accomplishment that was!

We may forget little things like car keys and anniversaries, but we remember precisely where and when we saw and heard our first white-throated sparrows. It was on a crisp, frosty morning in our first autumn of birding. We were walking around a community garden plot where weeds had gone to seed, and there we surprised a flock of birds feeding industriously. We knew at once that they were sparrows, but not ordinary sparrows. Their brightly striped heads and yellow lores made them something special.

The birds flew up into a thicket and remained quiet while we studied their field marks, then the field guide. We had just matched them up with their picture when one of them tuned up and sang. Even the song, we were amazed to discover, was clearly described in the field guide: a high, lyrical, "Poor Sam Peabody, Peabody, Peabody!"

We savored every syllable, marveling that we had lived so many years without having heard the song before.

Within a few years Ted began to miss some of these syllables, and then at last all the notes were lost—and we could share only the memory. I stopped telling him when I heard it, rather than remind him of what he was missing.

Then we were granted a strange reprieve.

We were in Maine, on vacation. It was June and the songs of nesting birds filled the air. Outside our cottage, a white-throated sparrow proclaimed his territory in a low, husky voice, like the sound of a record played at slow speed. The notes were right, but the tempo was wrong, and the high, lyrical quality was missing. I thought it odd for a bird in this northern country to speak with a southern drawl. Was this the way white-throats were supposed to sing on their nesting grounds? I wondered about it but said nothing.

I didn't need to. Ted heard it, loud and clear, and his face lit up with the joy of recognition. He was hearing a familiar voice from the past.

Other white-throats around us began to sing in their normal tones. Only this one, for reasons we will never know, lowered its pitch so that it was audible to both of us, and so throughout that brief vacation we were able to share its music.

I think about that one special white-throat now as I look forward to the Christmas Count, when I am likely to tally more than 200 of its kind. I will be marking, without comment, all the little "zeets" heard in the dark before dawn, and during the day I may stop to listen to the familiar "Sam Peabody" song that is sung, sometimes, even in the cold of December. It is romantic and totally unrealistic to hope that one eccentric white-throat will lower his voice an octave and sing a song we both can hear.

PART SEVEN

Messengers of Comfort and Joy

A Summer without a Swallow

FROM THE TONE OF THE VOICE ON THE TELEPHONE, I COULD not be sure whether I was the recipient of a complaint or merely an announcement.

"Some birds have built a nest on my porch."

Was he holding me personally responsible because of my acknowledged connection with the Audubon Naturalist Society? I waited for elaboration.

"I don't know what they are," the stranger continued, and now I recognized the plaintive note as puzzlement. "I've never seen birds like this before."

Identification was what he wanted. I wondered what rare species he might be entertaining and guessed, ahead of the description, that they might be house finches, which seem to baffle a good many people.

My guess was wrong.

"They have glossy, purplish-blue backs and long forked tails, and they've built a nest of mud and straw under the awning on my porch."

Seldom is identification by telephone so easy.

"You have barn swallows," I told him, restraining the impulse to add a hearty "Congratulations!" I was still not sure how he felt about his guests.

He felt fine about them—had, in fact, changed his way of life, as many of us have done, in honor of nesting birds. There were young birds in the nest, he said; both parents were feeding them, and he didn't want to do anything to disrupt the process.

"We don't use the front door now," he said. "We keep it locked and watch the birds from the window. But I'm afraid someone coming up on the porch might scare them away."

He was relieved to hear that barn swallows are quite tolerant of humans, and I was relieved to know that my caller was tolerant of swallows on his premises. More than tolerant, he was downright protective. Unlike many Harry Homeowner types who call me, he expressed no concern over the mess that a family of birds might make. That concern might come later, when the parents toilet-trained the youngsters, teaching them to perch, tails out, on the edge of the nest, and thus keep their own quarters neat and tidy. Meanwhile (although my caller had not observed this), the parents were keeping the nest neat and tidy themselves, carrying fecal material off to a distant dumping ground. Their beaks were always loaded: with food on the way to the nest, with refuse when they left it.

We did not discuss this aspect of swallow rearing. My caller had other questions on his mind. How long would it be before the young would learn to fly? And after they were launched, how long would they continue to use the nest?

He was surprised to learn that the young, once they have left the nest, never return. But he decided to leave it undisturbed when I told him that the adults might patch it up and use it again to raise their second brood. He was happy to hear that. This man who had never before seen a barn swallow was looking forward to a

Swallows

whole summer of swallow watching. No inconvenience of access and egress was too great a price to pay for this privilege. He and his family would continue to use the back door as long as necessary.

Leaving the phone, I marveled that anyone could grow up in the continental United States without ever encountering barn swallows, for they appear in every state, ranging as far north as Alaska. During migration, they flock together on utility wires in numbers sufficient to attract the attention of the most casual observers. During the nesting season, they make themselves at home in cities and suburbs as well as in rural areas, building their nests on porches, under eaves, in carports and garages, sometimes under bridges.

Barn swallows don't require barns, but a barn without them is a lonely place, as I learned at an early age. When goldenrods bloomed and school opened for the fall, the colony of swallows that had spent the summer darting in and out of the barn was suddenly and mysteriously gone. I didn't know that they had departed for South America, and that they might travel as far as Argentina. I knew only that the barn was depressingly empty.

Throughout the summer I felt their companionable presence. In the spring I had watched them at work building their nests, patiently gathering moist mud and dry grass, and at the end of the process, soft chicken feathers to add the finishing touch to their decor, a luxury not available to city-dwelling swallows.

At milking time, their soft "whit, whit" accompanied the rhythmic "swish, swish" of the streams of milk striking the pail. On lazy summer days, their melodious twittering was my background music as I hid out in the hayloft with a favorite book.

Not only in the barn, but all over the farm they were in constant evidence, skimming gracefully over the surface of the pond to capture insects; flying low over the pasture where the cows grazed; and some of them, with a preference for the outdoors rather than the dim interior of the barn, constructing their nests on ledges under overhanging rocks along steep gullies.

They were as familiar as robins, and ten times as elegant. I loved their graceful flight, their quiet manner, their magnificent coloring. I thought I knew every detail of their markings, from the peach-colored underparts to the deeper rust of the forehead and throat, the masked eyes, the glistening purplish back, the long forked tail. But I was an adult before I discovered the delicate white band decorating the tail, like a row of lace added as a finishing touch.

I was traveling in Arizona when I made that belated discovery. Sitting in a strange motel room, I heard a quiet "Whit, whit, whit!" outside that took me right back to childhood and the old familiar barn. I had not expected to find barn swallows in Arizona, but there they were, like old friends far from home. They were fluttering around the porch lights catching insects, and the lights illuminated the white contrast on the tail. Strange that I had never noticed this before! Perhaps this was a feature of the southwestern race, missing in our eastern barn swallows.

That conjecture proved false. I had simply not observed as closely as I had thought. Now I take special delight in finding that added ornamentation on the familiar swallows that come and go across the street, where they have built a nest in my neighbor's carport. Fortunately, my neighbor, like the stranger on the phone, is hospitable to swallows. She, too, discovered them late in life.

Late discoveries are rewarding. But I can think of no reward adequate to compensate for all those summers without swallows.

Break the News with Eagles

No winter is complete for us without a pilgrimage to Blackwater Wildlife Refuge to see the thousands of geese that gather there. But on our last trip to Maryland's Eastern Shore, we found Blackwater like a ghost town. There was not a goose in sight, on the ground or in the air. Normally one can expect to see a few thousand before ever reaching the refuge, and to see thousands more in the fields surrounding the visitors' center.

There was something ominous about the deserted field. Surely they must have been visited by some devastating plague.

Alarmed, we asked the park ranger, "Where are all the geese?"

Her answer was comfortingly light-hearted. "Oh, they made pigs of themselves out in the fields last night, feeding by moonlight. Now they're stuffed and lazy, and sleeping it off out in the bay."

Even with that reassurance, it was eerie traveling around the wildlife drive without seeing the customary hordes of Canada and snow geese. It just wasn't Black-water.

But there were compensations. There were eagles, bald eagles, more than I had ever seen there before, and we laughed about coming to Blackwater and seeing more eagles than geese.

The first two flew up, only a few yards from the car, from a field that should have been full of grazing geese. They seemed to be engaged in combat, facing each other with talons out and wings flapping, and as they sparred in mid-air a third eagle appeared, circling widely around them as if refereeing the match.

That was only the beginning. Repeatedly we saw swarms of ducks take to the air, scared up from their peaceful ponds by a low-flying eagle. On foot and in the car, we continued to see eagles in the air, eagles perched on dead trees, and eagles sitting on the ground. From the observation tower we saw four of them lined up on a muddy peninsula, feeding on fish at the water's edge.

This was an experience I would have to share with my younger brother, who often calls me to report on his bird sightings along the Mississippi Flyway. I reflected on the good fortune of a family that grows up sharing an appreciation of nature. Separated by time and distance, we have little that we can share except the twice-told reminiscences of childhood. The seven of us, reared in Illinois farm country, have gone in seven different directions, and without this one common link we could quickly run out of safe topics for conversation when we get together, and our letters could easily become mere health bulletins with the advancing years.

Far more satisfying are the reports from a sister who has sighted wild turkeys on her farm in Maryland, and the one in the midwest who has staked out a den of foxes, and yet another who flushes bobwhites on her daily walks. The brother in the east reports on the arrival and departure of the swans that winter on his river, and the family members who stayed in the midwest report on the migration dates of ducks and geese along the Mississippi.

I share news of my field trips with all of them. But when I think of eagles, I think of my younger brother and the unexpected phone call from him about this time two years ago. As it happened, it interrupted the evening news, just as we were about to hear the latest statistics on smoking and lung cancer. It didn't matter. I knew the statistics well enough. What my brother had to say was more important.

He was talking about bald eagles, in great numbers.

"I was just thinking about you," he said, "and how you'd enjoy the sight of all those eagles feeding in the river below the dam. As I came across the bridge from Keokuk this afternoon, I saw twenty of them in one tree, and then I kept seeing more, out over the river and along the shore, eating fish—the most we've ever had here. I counted more than a hundred."

More than a hundred bald eagles at one time! I could scarcely imagine it. I was lucky to see two or three in a year, for all the hours I was spending in the field with binoculars, and I thought of all the people in this country who have never seen even one, except on television.

We talked hopefully that night of the survival prospects of this endangered species, and then the topic switched, smoothly and casually, to the reason for my brother's trip across the river, and the real reason for this call.

He had been over at the hospital for a checkup, he said. . . .

With one ear, I was hearing the newscaster's voice in the next room reciting the grim statistics, and with the other ear I was hearing a live statistic. My brother, a chainsmoker for years, had a tumor on his right lung. He was to have surgery on Monday.

It was all unreal. But not to my brother. Realistically, methodically, he was clearing his desk, updating his will, putting his personal affairs in order, and informing the scattered family, beginning with me.

In the months of his convalescence, I often thought of his concern for the survival of the bald eagles when his own survival was in question, and of his capacity for enjoyment of the scene in spite of personal disaster. He even joked about the eagles. "We may have to chase them away," he said. "They're eating all our catfish!"

Writing to him later that night, I commented on his novel approach to breaking bad news. It would serve as an example when my own turn came. I would try to remember to introduce the topic with eagles—lots of eagles.

I didn't call to tell him about the eagles at Blackwater. He might think it was only an introduction to a tale of catastrophe. And besides, what is a dozen eagles to a man who has seen more than a hundred at a time?

Miracles Happen in Migration

"Nothing wholly admirable ever happens in this country," declared the late Brooks Atkinson, former drama critic for the *New York Times*, "except the migration of birds."

A bold statement, that, even for a drama critic. My husband and I have reexamined it from time to time but have found no evidence to challenge it, in its totality. In any case, we are agreed, after years of birding together, that the migration of birds is wholly admirable. And so each year we take time out in spring and fall, turn our backs on the unadmirable events that darken the pages of the daily papers and mar the serenity of our daily lives, and for a few days devote our full attention to the birds in their epic struggle against the unfriendly forces of nature.

Our autumn ritual takes us to Cape May, New Jersey, where the days go by all too quickly. It was at the end of our last pilgrimage that we encountered the most remarkable sight we had ever witnessed in all our years of following the migration. It was nothing short of miraculous, and we were the only witnesses.

We have thought since that we were negligent not to report it to the *New York Times*, which does take note of such events. It would have presented a bright accent note amid the stories of human violence and economic disaster. And it would have been strikingly dramatic on the evening news, "in living color." But miracles are short-lived; they cannot wait for camera crews.

It happened in a small resort town on the New Jersey coast. We were heading north from Cape May, feeling a little sad at ending this annual respite. For us, the big show was over and it was back to the real world again. En route, we consoled ourselves with memories of all the little warblers flitting about in quest of their last meal before taking off over the Atlantic; of great flights of herons and egrets against sunset clouds; of a sky filled with sharp-shinned hawks, and the air filled with the cries of bluejays.

We remembered most of all the overwhelming numbers of swallows swooping down over the lighthouse pond at Cape May Point, to take quick sips of water or to catch insects in passing. Seen from a distance, they looked like swarming insects themselves, in great dark clouds.

They were mostly tree swallows, their white underparts twinkling in the sunlight as they swirled overhead. When they dipped down, sometimes missing our heads only by inches, we could see that the majority of them were immature, distinguished by their dusky backs. It became a kind of game to spot the adults, with their iridescent blue-green backs, and to estimate their numbers. It was a game, too, to search the flocks for late-migrating barn swallows or an occasional purple martin, most of which were already well on their way down the coast.

On the first day of our trip we had seen weary swallows everywhere: clustered in trees on the roof-tops, on sandy beaches and on parking lots, and even on the highway, where many, too fatigued to move, were crushed by passing cars. On utility wires they huddled so closely together that the wires were invisible and the birds appeared to be suspended in mid-air by some feat of magic.

On the fourth day there was a change in weather, and the swallow flights diminished considerably. Now, as we drove north, there was not a single swallow to be seen, in the air or on the roadside wires. It appeared that the great mass movement was over.

But not yet. Suddenly, as we slowed down to enter the small town, one of those swirling bird-clouds appeared ahead of us, materializing out of nowhere.

We might not have noticed it if we had not been watching a lone woman walking down the deserted street from which all the summer people had fled. She could have been one of them, left behind by the flock, still in her brilliant summer plumage—an abbreviated sunback dress of vivid orange and yellow. She was teetering over the uneven pavement on high-heeled sandals, poorly designed to carry her weight.

With a week of intensive birding to sharpen our observation, we took note of her field marks and her lethargic behavior as she paused to light a cigarette.

It was then that we saw the swallows beyond her— thousands of them—fluttering, soaring, gliding, in shifting patterns of light and shadow against the mid-morning sky.

The woman in the foreground did not turn her head. But for us, such a performance was not to be ignored. We had been granted an encore, and we meant to enjoy it to the utmost.

We came to a full stop and watched through binoculars the milling confusion overhead. Out of that confusion a pattern emerged as groups of birds climbed upward, then in swift, graceful descent, swept down abruptly, disappearing briefly behind a row of buildings, then reappearing as they ascended once more on an invisible roller-coaster track to become a part of the milling mass again.

Their target, we surmised, must be a pond or a municipal swimming pool beyond the buildings that obscured our view, so we drove around the block and parked on the side street where we could see the entire scene.

What we found was not a pond or a pool, but an empty parking lot with a broad puddle of water left from the previous night's rain. The puddle was not more than an inch deep, but it was sufficient to meet the needs of some 5,000 thirsty travelers.

In a stunning display of close-drill formation and precision diving, they descended by turns, as confidently as if they were approaching a lake or pond. There was no confusion in the descent, no mid-air collisions, no bickering among the members of the flock. Each in turn took a drink from the shallow pool without touching the pavement, without even rippling the water.

We marveled at their orderly maneuvering and marveled too at their choice of this meager watering place. And as we marveled, the last swallow in the flock made its dive without our realizing it was the last. Suddenly the great milling flock was moving off, rapidly becoming one of those insect-like swarms against the sky.

Still dazed by the performance, we moved on, returning to the main highway. There was no one in sight until we caught up with the lone woman, still plodding along on her wobbly heels.

As we passed, she paused at the curb and without looking up took a final drag from her cigarette and flipped it into a rain-pool as shallow as the one that had attracted the thirsty swallows.

In the smoking of one cigarette, a miracle had taken place, and she would never know.

On Phoebes and Bridges

CHILDREN ON THEIR WAY TO SCHOOL TAKE A SHORTCUT through our woods, scuffing the dead leaves and hopping over fallen branches. Whose woods these are they may not know, or even care. They are too young to concern themselves with property rights and the technicalities of trespassing. They are also too young to have learned the axiom that the shortest distance between two points is a straight line between them. But they know about shortcuts.

Birds, too, take shortcuts across our property, stopping off only because it is on the direct line between a starting point and a destination. These are not the birds that are lured by our offerings. They come and go without visiting the feeders, although they may find special seed and insect treats of which we are not even aware. Of the ninety-two species we have seen here over the years, some we have seen only once, and only briefly before they went on their purposeful way.

Among these one-time visitors was an eastern phoebe

that appeared one March day. I happened to see it alight on the utility wire outside the window. It wagged its tail in typical phoebe fashion, balanced on the wire and perched there for fully two minutes, and then it was gone without uttering a sound. But it left a wake of childhood memories that lasted through the day as clouds gathered and a chill rain fell over the patches of snow that lingered at the edge of the woods.

On just such days as this, when I took unauthorized shortcuts across the fields on the way to school, wading through streams swollen by melting snow, I would hear the hoarse "fee-bee" call and trace it to an inconspicuous grayish bird that was usually found perched on a limb overhanging the water. It was so plain, so unassuming in dress and manner, that it could easily have been overlooked if it had not given that peculiar call, over and over.

Even today that repeated wheeze is associated in memory with the persistent calls of the tufted titmouse in the woods, the shattering of icicles, and the subdued sound of the creek running beneath a surface layer of ice.

I learned about phoebes from my father. "They like bridges," he told me.

I, too, liked bridges. I made paper canoes and dropped them carefully into the water on one side of the footbridge, then ran to the other side to see if they had survived the voyage without capsizing. I liked to wade under bridges and look up at their underpinnings to see if I could spot the nest of a phoebe or a barn swallow.

The phoebes came earlier, long before the first swallows. They came while the juncos were still hopping around in the snow. My father spoke of phoebes as "hardy little birds," admiring their ability to withstand the chill winds of Illinois in late February and March. They are surely the hardiest of the flycatchers, but I wonder about the ones that are brash enough to stay through the winter here in Maryland. We rarely fail to find at least one phoebe on the Christmas Count in mid-

December, ghost-like presences in shrubby shelter. These may be downright foolhardy. They have gambled on the weather, and they may lose. Their favorite fare of beetles and wasps and ants is hard to find in a normal winter; it is impossible in a winter of deep snow and crusted ice. It is far more comfortable to think of the phoebes arriving in the vanguard of spring, ahead of the first robins but not ahead of the first insects.

When other migrants are still far to the south, the phoebes are staking out their territories and selecting nesting sites—preferably near water, so the girders under bridges offer ideal locations, but rocky ledges on riverside cliffs are just as good. For all their modest appearance, phoebes are not really shy and do not shrink from human contact. They may even choose to build their neat mud-plaster nests on porches of houses, under eaves, or even on window sills.

But when I set out in the spring to look for the first phoebe, I go to the bridge where I have always found them nesting for the past seven years, where phoebes have probably been nesting since the bridge was built. And when I see the familiar phoebe perched on a branch near the bridge, I think of my father and his appreciation for this small, quiet bird.

The phoebe, I realize, has become something of a symbol to me, a link between two seasons and a link between two generations.

The youngsters who took a shortcut through my woods did not see my one and only phoebe the day it made its brief stopover. They were looking down, possibly contemplating the number and state of the dry leaves under their feet. Maybe they saw the clump of snowdrops by the path and got the same spring message from it that I got from the phoebe.

But I hope that some of those children have fathers or mothers who will tell them about the quiet phoebe and teach them to listen for its funny call, maybe even take them exploring to find its nest beneath the bridge.

The Last Life Bird

Loveliest of trees, the cherry now
Is hung with bloom along the bough . . .

WHY WOULD A. E. HOUSMAN'S LINES COME TO MIND ON
a lead-gray day in November when all the cherry trees
had lost their leaves?

It had been a dragging day, marked by high frustration and low achievement, a day with many tasks begun
and none of them completed.

The ring of the telephone at mid-afternoon signaled
one more unwelcome interruption. I resisted the strong
temptation to ignore it.

That call changed the tempo of the day, put priorities
in focus. It was not, as I expected, a plea for funds or
household castoffs, nor a pitch for a beach resort or a
cemetery plot.

It was a Rare Bird Alert, instantly raising my pulse
rate and setting the unofficial network into prompt action.

I recognized Ed's voice immediately, and the note of
excitement in it. He had just come back from Seneca,

he said, and he had to report two red-necked grebes on the river. He thought I would like to know and help spread the word.

Two red-necked grebes! I had seen only one in my life, ten years before. These were Ed's firsts. His pride was understandable.

Then, as if two red-necked grebes were not enough, he added three common loons, five oldsquaws, and a flock of white scoters mingling with a raft of ruddy ducks. He had struck a bonanza.

We talked briefly of birders' luck and how quickly the scene can change. Two days earlier we had shared a birding trip to Seneca and had found the river disappointingly barren. Ed, a long-time birding companion, usually full of zest and good spirits, had been low-key and subdued walking along beside me, and I feared he was ill. But now he was re-energized with the delight of his lone discovery, eager to share it with friends.

There was no question now of the day's priorities. After a half-dozen quick telephone calls I was on my way, feeling a joyful sense of liberation.

In the twenty-minute drive out River Road to Seneca, there was time to think of the projects left behind, all relatively unimportant in the scheme of life. It was then that I thought of Housman's poem, which we tack on the bulletin board each spring as our justification—no, our obligation—to leave windows unwashed and gutters uncleaned in favor of going afield to enjoy the transitory beauties of the season.

> *Now, of my threescore years and ten,*
> *Twenty will not come again,*
> *And take from seventy springs a score,*
> *It only leaves me fifty more.*
>
> *And since to look at things in bloom*
> *Fifty springs are little room,*
> *About the woodlands I will go*
> *to see the cherry hung with snow.*

It is a young man's song, written in the spring of life; but in this season of falling leaves it takes on a new urgency for those who are counting diminishing autumns.

The words came back to me again a few days later, on another lead-gray day when we gathered at the funeral chapel. Around me were some of the same friends who had answered my call and joined me that afternoon at Seneca.

There, standing on the riverbank, we had enjoyed the spirit of camaraderie as we quickly located the old-squaws and the ruddy ducks, sleeping at anchor. The scoters, as if to underscore the message of the fleeting

Red-necked Grebes

moment, had already departed, but Ed's three loons did a graceful flyby for our benefit before disappearing into the murky distance.

To our great relief, the prize birds were still there, and we spent a leisurely half-hour gazing through our telescopes at the serene picture of the two red-necked grebes floating in close tandem on the still waters of the Potomac.

In the chapel, we reflected on that tranquil scene as we listened to the eulogies and rejoiced for Ed, a good friend who had been granted, in the final week of a rewarding life, the special joy of discovering a life bird and passing the word to comrades.

We rejoiced, too, in the remembrance that all of us had dropped pressing chores that day to go out and share Ed Solotar's find, his last gift to us.

Everyday Wonders

WHEN FRIENDS COME HOME FROM THEIR FAR-FLUNG TRAV-
els with pictures of cathedrals and ruins and street ba-
zaars, my husband always asks, "How many birds did
you see?"

It is not a frivolous question. He has learned that
interest in birds adds zest to travel, even when birds
are not the primary focus of the trip. But his question
is usually answered with blank looks. People who travel
for a tourist's-eye view rarely see any birds at all, except
perhaps the pigeons in St. Mark's Square.

He has a favorite follow-up for those who confess to
a birdless vacation: "You mean you traveled through
six countries without seeing a single bird? Incredible!"

It should not be incredible to him. He knows people
who have driven this nation's highways for thirty years
without ever seeing a turkey vulture. And he should
remember our experience in walking across the Chesapeake Bay Bridge, along with 40,000 other pedestrians,
the day before it opened to vehicular traffic for the sea-

son. As we neared the east end of the bridge, we saw a late-migrating loon flying directly over the span on his lone way north.

We alone of all the thousands on the bridge stopped to watch his purposeful flight, following him with our binoculars until his identity was no longer distinguishable. Then we continued on our way, exhilarated at having seen something splendid that everyone else had missed.

Even on the C&O towpath, where people go to be close to nature, we are bypassed by countless hikers, bikers, and joggers whenever we stop to look at a special bird. One bright autumn day we were watching a family of bluebirds in a nearly bare sycamore across the canal when we caught a glimpse in our binoculars of something even more exciting. Beyond the bluebirds, high above the trees, was a kettle of red-tailed hawks. We counted sixteen of them, circling and soaring on their migration route, highlighted by the sun against a flawless blue sky, their tails flashing a red to match that of the maples beneath them. And beneath the trees, heedless throngs went on their way while we stood and watched a spectacular event.

Moments like that are meant to be shared. But often I have the feeling of being the sole witness to a significant happening. It comes to me in the fall when no one else at the shopping center is remotely aware of the steady stream of bluejays overhead; and in the spring, when blackpoll warblers, bringing up the rear of the migration in a massive overnight invasion, sing their songs unnoticed along every tree-lined street. Hidden by late spring foliage, they are heard more than seen, but on foot or in the car I can count their numbers by their voices, and I marvel at the number of people who pass by, unaware that something tremendous is happening.

It is the same in any season. Only yesterday when I was leaving the public library, I came to an abrupt halt at the loud, ringing call of a Carolina wren. Following the direction of his voice, I scanned the low bushes at the edge of the parking lot. As I stood quietly, waiting for a movement to reveal him, I realized that people were hurrying past me on their way to or from their cars without even stopping to listen.

The wren sang again, in marvelously clear, penetrating tones. Still no one stopped.

It was incredible, but of all that crowd, no one had heard him but me. No one else saw him as he emerged at the base of the shrub, all warm-brown-and-buff in the late afternoon sun. He flitted quickly to a nearby sapling and repeated his song so energetically that his throat swelled and his little tail quivered.

He was singing for an audience of one. Fifty people had missed the opportunity to see and hear a star performance.

These things happen all the time to those of us whose eyes and ears are turned on to birds. Above the chatter of human voices, above the noise of traffic, even above the scream of jets at an airport, we hear a familiar call and stop to listen. It is as if we are members of a great secret society, picking up signals that are invisible and inaudible to the average human.

I had the same feeling earlier in the week on a routine trip to the supermarket. As soon as I opened the car door, I heard a soft, sibilant chorus that drew my attention to a large flock of cedar waxwings in a hawthorn hedge alongside the parking lot. There were easily seventy-five of them, feeding enthusiastically on berries, as oblivious to the shoppers as the shoppers were to them.

I got back into the car and watched through the windshield as they shifted restlessly back and forth, as if searching for the tree with the biggest, sweetest berries. Cars came and went, but none of them stopped or even hesitated alongside the busy hedge, and dozens of people missed the rare opportunity to see these elegant birds at close range, without even the need for binoculars.

The urge to share was overwhelming. I wished that I were eccentric enough to jump from the car and stop traffic, to call attention to this extraordinary sight. But I am neither young enough nor old enough to yield to such an impulse. So I sat in silence absorbing the scene, grateful that my eyes and ears are turned on, and that I need travel no farther than to the grocery store to find adventure.

INDEX